T5-AOI-314

Didax
SKILLS SERIES

EDITING

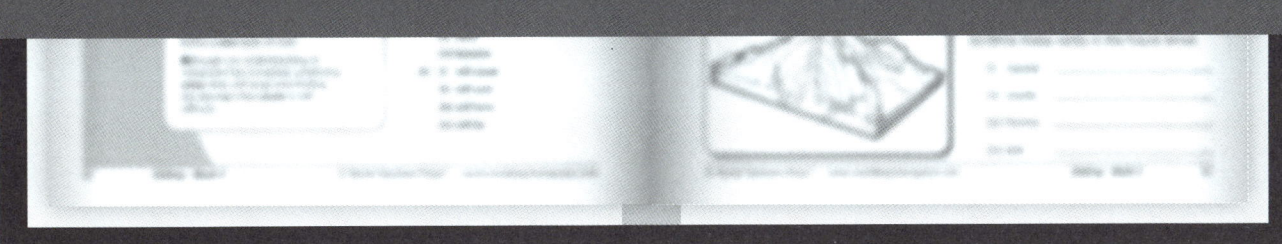

GRADES 3-4

Published with the permission of R.I.C. Publications Pty. Ltd.

Copyright © 2007 by Didax, Inc., Rowley, MA 01969. All rights reserved.

First published by R.I.C. Publications Pty. Ltd., Perth, Western Australia. Revised by Didax Educational Resources.

Limited reproduction permission: The publisher grants permission to individual teachers who have purchased this book to reproduce the blackline masters as needed for use with their own students. Reproduction for an entire school or school district or for commercial use is prohibited.

Printed in the United States of America.

Order Number: 2-5280
ISBN-13: 978-1-58324-262-9

A B C D E F 11 10 09 08 07

395 Main Street
Rowley, MA 01969
www.didax.com

Foreword

Editing consists of a selection of texts written in specific formats to provide punctuation, spelling and grammatical practice. Detailed descriptions of concepts, such as specific parts of speech and punctuation, are also included, as well as vocabulary enrichment and aspects of writing.

The aim is to provide students with varied, structured experiences in proofreading and editing written texts. A high level of proficiency in these skills is vital for accurate self-monitoring of written work.

Other titles in this series are:
- *Editing, Grades 2 to 3*
- *Editing, Grades 5 to 6*
- *Editing, Grades 7 to 8*

Contents

Teacher Information

Teacher Information	4–5
Overview of Activity Content	6–7
Punctuation, Spelling and Grammar Information	8–9
Writing Format Information	10–11
Writing Format Checklists	12–18
Student Proofreading and Editing Checklist	19

Worksheets

The Blue Whale	20–21	The Trojan Horse	62–63
Peep Loses Sheep	22–23	Pottery Place	64–65
Snake Bites	24–25	Monkeynaut	66–67
Chocolate	26–27	The Bear and the Tourists	68–69
The Wind and the Sun	28–29	How Plants Drink	70–71
Coconut Cookies	30–31	My Pop	72–73
Alaskan Vacation	32–33	Biography of Sir Edmund Hillary	74–75
Pet Parade	34–35	Kakadu National Park	76–77
The Gecko	36–37	Water and the Body	78–79
Fish for Classroom Pets	38–39	My Dance Trophy	80–81
The Egg and Bottle Experiment	40–41	Make-a-Face Flip Book	82–83
Explorer's Diary	42–43	Too Many Dogs	84–85
The Beach	44–45	Sabre-Toothed Cat	86–87
Elephants Can Fly	46–47	Life Cycle of a Butterfly	88–89
How a Thermometer Works	48–49	Save Our Water	90–91
Using a Washing Machine	50–51	Black Mamba	92–93
My Siamese Cat	52–53	A Warrior Queen's Dilemma	94–95
Wonderwings	54–55	Pennies and Pencils	96–97
Swimming Gold!	56–57	The Curse of the Mummy	98–99
Dinosaur Feast	58–59	The Storm	100–101
Volcanoes	60–61	Drink Water	102–103

Teacher Information

The following is an explanation of how to use the pages in this book.

Teacher Pages

A teacher page accompanies each student worksheet. It provides the following information:

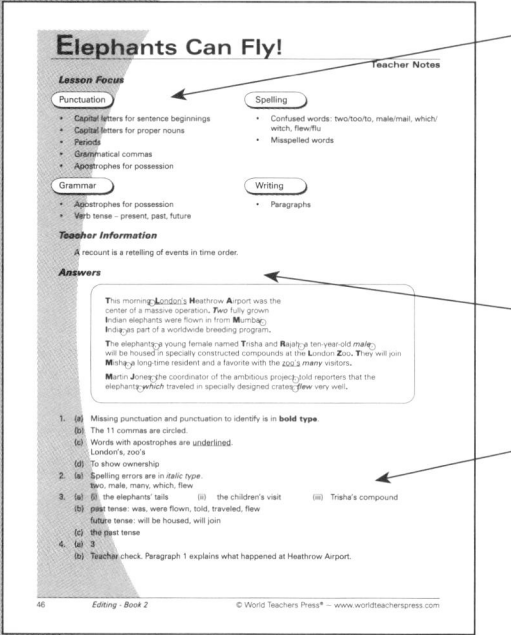

The Lesson Focus indicates the focus for each student page. This will include aspects from the areas of punctuation, spelling, grammar, vocabulary and writing. Some of these may involve simple recognition of a concept, or use an already-known aspect. More detailed teacher information about punctuation, spelling and grammar can be found on pages 8–9.

Teacher Information gives brief background information about each text type. More detailed information can be found on pages 10–11.

Answers to all worksheet activities are provided. The corrected text is given with punctuation errors in bold. Correct spelling is highlighted in italics, as well as being provided in the answers section.

Proofreading and Editing Marks

Editors use a number of consistent symbols to indicate where changes are to be made in a text.

Teachers may require students to use these "professional" proofreading and editing marks to indicate errors in the text on the student pages.

∧ = **insert (something)**

　The weather hot
　The boys hat
　He went swim ng.

/ = **delete (something)**

　I went to to the shops.
　The dog broke it's collar.

/ + *lc* = **lower case**

　I don't like Math.

≡ + *cap.* = **capital letter**

　"I'm telling mom."

/ + *correction* = **spelling**

　He wos playing football.

Teacher Information

Student Pages

- A specific text type is identified and presented for the students to read. The text has punctuation and spelling errors, as well as grammatical features for the student to identify, as specified by the worksheet or teacher.

- The texts are presented in two ways. One allows students to become familiar with formats they may encounter in some standardized tests; both follow a similar format for identifying and correcting proofreading and editing errors.

The student activities follow a common format.

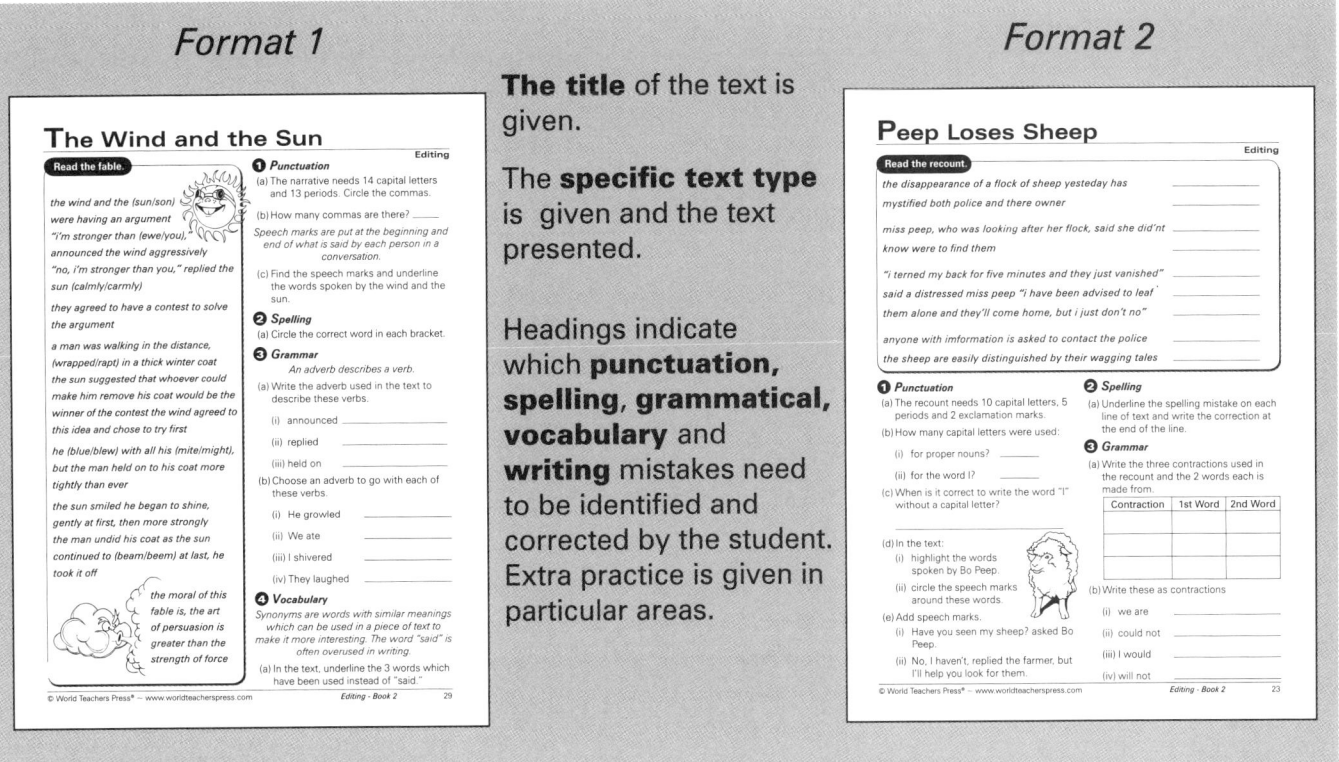

Student instructions are written in a consistent format to encourage students to concentrate on the activity.

Where an instruction requires students to "**find** capital letters, etc.," teachers should select their own method for students to use; for example, circle, highlight with a colored marker, underline or write over the error. Some proofreading and editing marks may be used. (See Teacher Notes page 4.)

Activity Content Overview

Page Number

Activity Content	21	23	25	27	29	31	33	35	37	39	41	43	45	47	49	51	53	55	57	59	61	63	65	67	69	71	73	75	77	79	81	83	85	87	89	91	93	95	97	99	101	103
PUNCTUATION																																										
Periods	•	•	•	•	•	•	•	•	•	•		•	•	•	•	•	•	•	•	•	•	•	•	•	•	•	•	•	•	•		•	•	•	•	•	•	•	•	•		•
Capital letters: begin. of sentences	•	•	•	•	•	•	•	•	•	•		•	•	•	•	•	•	•	•	•	•	•	•	•	•	•	•	•	•	•		•	•	•	•	•	•	•	•	•		•
proper nouns		•					•		•								•				•			•					•													
the pronoun "I"		•			•																																					
titles																												•			•											
Question marks	•									•																																
Exclamation marks	•	•						•			•							•	•							•																
Apostrophes: contractions							•	•										•									•															
possession				•																							•				•											
Commas: in a list					•		•			•				•			•				•							•														
grammatical				•	•		•			•	•	•	•		•		•	•			•			•	•	•		•														
Direct speech	•																								•							•								•	•	
Colons: recognition			•																																							
SPELLING																																										
Misspelled words		•			•		•			•		•	•	•	•	•	•	•		•	•	•		•		•		•	•	•		•	•	•	•	•	•	•	•	•	•	•
Confused words		•			•		•			•			•		•	•	•	•		•	•	•				•	•	•	•	•		•	•			•				•		
Plurals: adding "s" and "es"																							•																			
change "y" to "i"																																				•						
Suffixes: drop silent "e"																										•									•				•			
doubling consonants																																										
change "y" to "i"	•																																									
Silent letters																			•				•				•	•														
TEXT TYPE	Rep.	Rec.	P	D	N	P	Rec.	N	D	Expo.	P/Expl.	Rec.	D	Rec.	Expl.	P	D	Expo.	Rec.	N	Expl.	Rec.	P	Rec.	N	Expl.	D	Rec.	Rep.	Expl.	D	P	Expo.	Rep.	Expl.	Expo.	Rep.	N	Rep.	Rec.	N	Expo.

Activity Content | Page Number

Activity Content	21	23	25	27	29	31	33	35	37	39	41	43	45	47	49	51	53	55	57	59	61	63	65	67	69	71	73	75	77	79	81	83	85	87	89	91	93	95	97	99	101	103
GRAMMAR																																										
Nouns: common nouns			•																			•													•							
collective nouns	•																																									
Pronouns													•										•					•										•				•
Adjectives			•	•				•	•								•		•	•					•		•										•		•	•	•	
Comparative and superlative	•										•																															
Verbs			•		•						•																															
Verb tenses																	•			•							•	•		•						•		•				
Adverbs					•																				•													•				
Conjunctions									•	•																•				•												
Contractions		•						•	•								•			•							•										•					
Apostrophes: possession															•												•															
Indefinite article: "a" or "an"															•																	•										
VOCABULARY																																										
Enrichment																									•		•	•		•						•						•
Synonyms														•								•								•					•							
Antonyms								•										•															•			•			•			
Compound words										•			•																												•	
Similes																													•													
Shortened forms						•							•																								•					
WRITING																																										
Paragraphs																							•																•			
Sentences																												•														
TEXT TYPE	Rep.	Rec.	P	D	N	P	Rec.	N	D	Expo.	P/Expl.	Rec.	D	Rec.	Expl.	P	D	Expo.	Rec.	N	Expl.	Rec.	P	Rec.	N	Expl.	D	Rec.	Rep.	Expl.	D	P	Expo.	Rep.	Expl.	Expo.	Rep.	N	Rep.	Rec.	N	Expo.

Narrative – N   Explanation – Expl.   Procedure – P   Recount – Rec.   Report – Rep.   Exposition – Expo.   Description – D

Teacher Information
Punctuation, Spelling and Grammar Information

PUNCTUATION

Please note: In some cases, teachers will need to exercise their own judgment with regard to punctuation, as certain aspects, particularly commas and exclamation marks, are to an extent discretionary and depend on the individual writer's intent.

Capital Letters

Capital letters are needed for:
- *sentence beginnings*; e.g., My dog is very friendly. He welcomes everyone.
- *proper nouns* – people's names (Chloe Parker), names of places (Indian Ocean), days of the week (Saturday), months (December), holidays and festivals (Christmas), countries (America), nationalities (Russian), languages (Italian) and religions (Buddhism).
- *titles*; e.g., World Health Organization

Commas

Commas are used to separate items in a list or series.

I enjoy reading, playing squash, skiing and swimming.

Grammatical commas are used to:
- make the meaning of a sentence clear.

    Jane said her mother is very busy.　　(Jane's mother is very busy.)
    Jane, said her mother, is very busy.　　(Jane is very busy.)

- indicate where a pause is needed in a sentence.

    Many years ago, dinosaurs roamed the Earth.

Apostrophes for Possession

Apostrophes are used to show that something belongs to someone or something.

The placement of the apostrophe can be challenging but the simple rule is that it is placed after the owner or owners. (The "tail" of the apostrophe "points" to the owner[s].)

the boy's shoes　　(one boy)　　the boys' shoes　　(more than one boy)
the lady's hats　　(one lady)　　the ladies' hats　　(more than one lady)

Contractions

Contractions are words that have been made by joining and shortening two words. An apostrophe is used in place of the missing letters.

would not　　wouldn't　　will not　　won't
I would　　I'd　　they are　　they're

SPELLING

Singular and plural nouns

Adding "s" and "es"

The most commonly used plural is made by adding "s"; e.g., books, games.

It is usually necessary to add "es" to nouns ending in "ch," "sh," "s," "x" and "z" to make the plural easier to pronounce; e.g., washes, dishes, classes, foxes and waltzes.

Adding "s" and "es" continued

Words ending in "o" are also often made into a plural by adding "es."

　　potatoes, tomatoes

Teacher Information

There are many exceptions, including radios, merinos, silos, zeros, photos and sopranos.
Students should be encouraged to consult a dictionary if uncertain about the spelling of a certain word.

GRAMMAR

Nouns
Nouns are naming words of people, places and things; e.g., teacher, school, desk.
Proper nouns name individual people (Bill), places (Kings Park) and others (Christmas, December, Sunday). Proper nouns are written with capital letters.
Common nouns are any other nouns.
Collective nouns are a subset of common nouns; e.g., a team of players.

Pronouns
A *pronoun* is a word substituted for a noun; e.g., *They* asked *him* to help *them*.
Personal pronouns refer to you, me and other people; e.g., I, me, you, she, us, them, etc.

Adjectives
Adjectives modify (enhance or change) the meaning of nouns and, less commonly, pronouns; e.g., *parched* land; *green, fertile* land; *poor old* me; *lucky* you.

Verbs
Verbs are "doing" words; e.g., swim, like, look.
Auxiliary verbs join other verbs to form verb groups; e.g., have eaten, will be asleep.
Verb tense. There are three basic tenses. Because there are so many irregular verbs in English, tense can be complex.

	the past .... *the present* .... *the future*
regular	played .... play .... will play has played .... plays .... should play
irregular	went .... go .... will go has gone .... goes .... should go

NOTE: The future and the past tenses often use auxiliary verbs.

Adverbs
Adverbs are words that modify (enhance on change) the meaning of verbs.

    He ran *quickly*.   I've seen this *before*.

There are adverbs of:
- time   e.g. yesterday
- place   e.g. downstairs
- manner   e.g. carefully

Conjunctions
Conjunctions are joining words. They can join different language units.
- One word with another   e.g., black *or* white
- One phrase with another   e.g., on the beach *and* in the sand
- One clause with another   e.g., He asked me *if* I could cook.
- One sentence with another   e.g., I was hot *so* I went for a swim.

Teacher Information

Writing Format Information

Below are general descriptions of the text types included in this book.

Narrative

- is a framework which tells a story.
- includes:
  - *Orientation:*
    the setting, time and character(s)
  - *Complication:*
    involving the main character(s) and a sequence of events.
  - *Resolution:*
    to the complication
  - *Ending:*
    often showing what has changed and what the characters have learned.
- uses:
  - a range of conjunctions to connect ideas
  - appropriate paragraphing
  - descriptive language
  - past tense.

A narrative may be written in the form of a poem, story, play, imaginative story, fairy tale, novel, myth, legend, ballad, science fiction story, or modern fantasy.

Report

- is a framework which describes aspects of a living or nonliving thing in detail.
- includes:
  - *Classification:*
    a general or classifying statement
  - *Description:*
    accurate and detailed
  - *Conclusion:*
    a comment about the content of the report (optional).
- uses:
  - factual language rather than imaginative
  - the third person
  - the timeless present tense
  - linking and action verbs.

A report may be written in the form of a book review, scientific report, newspaper or magazine article, eyewitness account, or a progress report.

Recount

- is a framework that retells events as they happened in time order.
- may be factual, personal, or imaginative.
- includes:
  - *Orientation:*
    all relevant background (who, when, where, why)
  - *Events:*
    significant events in detail
  - *Conclusion:*
    often with an evaluative comment.
- uses:
  - vocabulary to suggest time passing
  - paragraphs to show separate sections
  - the past tense.

A recount may be written in the form of a newspaper report, diary, letter, journal, eyewitness account, biography, autobiography, or history.

Procedure

- is a framework which outlines how something is made or done.
- includes:
  - the purpose of the procedure shown clearly and precisely
  - a list of materials or requirements under appropriate headings or layout
  - the method in a detailed, logical sequence
  - an evaluation (if appropriate).
- uses:
  - instructions with an imperative verb
  - subject-specific vocabulary
  - simple present tense.

A procedure may be written in the form of a recipe, instructions for making something, an experiment, an instruction manual, a math procedure, how to play a game, how to operate an appliance, how to use an atlas and how to deal with a problem.

Teacher Information

Writing Format Information

Exposition

- is a framework which argues for a particular position and attempts to persuade the audience to share this view.
- includes:
  - *Introduction:* statement of the problem and the writer's position
  - *Arguments:* presented in a logical manner with supporting detail, usually from the strongest to the weakest
  - *Conclusion:* an evaluation restating the writer's position.
- uses:
  - persuasive language
  - paragraphs to state and elaborate on each point.

An exposition may be written in the form of an essay, a letter, a policy statement, a critical review, an advertisement, an editorial, or a speech.

Explanation

- is a framework which outlines how something occurs, works, or is made.
- includes:
  - *Statement:* precisely what is to be explained
  - *Explanation:* a clear account in logical sequence of how and why the phenomenon occurs
  - *Conclusion:* an evaluation and comment about what has been explained.

  OR

  - a definition
  - a description of the components or parts
  - the operation—how it works or is made
  - the application—where and when it works or is applied
  - special features—interesting comments
  - evaluation or comment.
- uses:
  - subject–specific terms and technical vocabulary where appropriate
  - simple present tense
  - linking words to show cause and effect.

An explanation may be written in the form of an essay, a handbook (for example, how a kite works), a science text, a health text, or a social studies text.

Description

- is a framework which describes specific living or nonliving things.

Physical characteristics of living things are described; nonliving things are described in terms of their components and/or their functions. Special features are also discussed. This type of writing can be used to describe, for example, a specific breed of animal, an object, or a picture.

- includes:
  - *Introduction:* what it is
  - *Description:* its appearance (color, shape, size, etc.)
  - *Interesting details/special features*
  - *Concluding statement.*
- uses:
  - adjectives extensively
  - joining words.

A description may be written in poetic form and may describe a person, place, animal, thing, or emotion.

Writing Format Checklists

Student Narrative Checklist

Title: _____

Orientation:
My title is interesting. ☐
I introduced the characters. ☐
I said where they were. ☐
I said when the story happened. ☐

Complication:
I told about the problem. ☐
I told about the events that happened. ☐

Resolution:
I told how they solved the problem. ☐

Ending:
My story has a suitable ending. ☐
I used interesting words. ☐
My story made sense. ☐

Name: _____ Date: _____

Student Narrative Checklist

Title: _____

Orientation:
My title is interesting. ☐
I introduced the characters. ☐
I said where they were. ☐
I said when the story happened. ☐

Complication:
I told about the problem. ☐
I told about the events that happened. ☐

Resolution:
I told how they solved the problem. ☐

Ending:
My story has a suitable ending. ☐
I used interesting words. ☐
My story made sense. ☐

Name: _____ Date: _____

Writing Format Checklists

Student Recount Checklist

☐

☐ ☐ ☐

☐ ☐

☐ ☐ ☐

Title:

My title is suitable.

Orientation:

I told who was there.
I told when it happened.
I told where it happened.

Events:

I gave details about the events.
The events were in the correct order.

Ending:

I said how it ended
and how I felt about it.
My recount made sense.

Name: _____ Date: _____

Student Recount Checklist

☐

☐ ☐ ☐

☐ ☐

☐ ☐ ☐

Title:

My title is suitable.

Orientation:

I told who was there.
I told when it happened.
I told where it happened.

Events:

I gave details about the events.
The events were in the correct order.

Ending:

I said how it ended
and how I felt about it.
My recount made sense.

Name: _____ Date: _____

Writing Format Checklists

Student Exposition Checklist

Title: _____

Overview:
- I stated the topic. ☐
- I said what I thought about it. ☐

Arguments:
- I explained my ideas about the topic. ☐
- I started with my strongest argument. ☐
- I provided information to support my arguments. ☐
- I used persuasive language. ☐

Conclusion:
- I summed up my arguments. ☐
- My exposition makes sense. ☐
- Other people will understand my arguments. ☐

Name: _____   Date: _____

Student Exposition Checklist

Title: _____

Overview:
- I stated the topic. ☐
- I said what I thought about it. ☐

Arguments:
- I explained my ideas about the topic. ☐
- I started with my strongest argument. ☐
- I provided information to support my arguments. ☐
- I used persuasive language. ☐

Conclusion:
- I summed up my arguments. ☐
- My exposition makes sense. ☐
- Other people will understand my arguments. ☐

Name: _____   Date: _____

Writing Format Checklists

Student Explanation Checklist

Title: ☐

Definition: ☐ ☐ ☐
I clearly stated what I was going to explain.

Description: ☐ ☐ ☐
I explained how it happens or works.
My information was in a logical order.
I explained things clearly.

Concluding statement:
I made an interesting comment or conclusion.
People will understand my explanation.
I included all the necessary information.

Name: _____ Date: _____

Student Explanation Checklist

Title: ☐

Definition: ☐ ☐ ☐
I clearly stated what I was going to explain.

Description: ☐ ☐ ☐
I explained how it happens or works.
My information was in a logical order.
I explained things clearly.

Concluding statement:
I made an interesting comment or conclusion.
People will understand my explanation.
I included all the necessary information.

Name: _____ Date: _____

Writing Format Checklists

Student Report Checklist

Title: _____

Classification:
I told what it is. ☐

Description:
I described it clearly. ☐
I included interesting facts. ☐

Conclusion:
I said what I thought about it. ☐
I used facts. ☐
My report was interesting. ☐

Name: _____ Date: _____

Student Report Checklist

Title: _____

Classification:
I told what it is. ☐

Description:
I described it clearly. ☐
I included interesting facts. ☐

Conclusion:
I said what I thought about it. ☐
I used facts. ☐
My report was interesting. ☐

Name: _____ Date: _____

Writing Format Checklists

Student Procedure Checklist

Title: _____

Goal: ☐
I said what I wanted to do or make.

Materials: ☐
I made a list of what was needed.

Steps: ☐ ☐ ☐
I explained the steps clearly.
The steps were in the right order.
I didn't leave out any steps.

Test: ☐ ☐ ☐
I said how it should look or work in the end.
I didn't use any unnecessary words.
Other people could follow my procedure.

Name: _____ **Date:** _____

Student Procedure Checklist

Title: _____

Goal: ☐
I said what I wanted to do or make.

Materials: ☐
I made a list of what was needed.

Steps: ☐ ☐ ☐
I explained the steps clearly.
The steps were in the right order.
I didn't leave out any steps.

Test: ☐ ☐ ☐
I said how it should look or work in the end.
I didn't use any unnecessary words.
Other people could follow my procedure.

Name: _____ **Date:** _____

Writing Format Checklists

Student Description Checklist

Title:

Introduction:
I said what it is. ☐

Description:
I told about its appearance. ☐
I told about any interesting details. ☐
I told about its special features. ☐
I used lots of different adjectives (describing words). ☐

Name: _____ Date: _____

Student Description Checklist

Title:

Introduction:
I said what it is. ☐

Description:
I told about its appearance. ☐
I told about any interesting details. ☐
I told about its special features. ☐
I used lots of different adjectives (describing words). ☐

Name: _____ Date: _____

Student Proofreading and Editing Checklist

Use this page to check your work. You will not need to check all of the boxes.

Name: _____   Date: _____

Title: _____

Punctuation:

I have included:

- capital letters for:
  - beginning sentences ☐
  - proper nouns ☐
  - titles ☐
- question marks ☐
- periods ☐
- commas:
  - in lists ☐
  - for pauses ☐
  - to make meaning clear ☐
- apostrophes:
  - for contractions ☐
  - to show ownership ☐
- exclamation marks ☐

Spelling:

I have:

- checked the spelling of any unknown words ☐
- not confused words that sound the same ☐

Grammar:

I have included:

- different "doing" words (verbs) ☐
- appropriate adverbs to describe verbs ☐
- suitable nouns (naming words) ☐
- appropriate pronouns ☐
- interesting adjectives (describing words) ☐
- suitable conjunctions (joining words) ☐

Writing:

I have read through my writing to check that:

- it makes sense ☐
- it is easy to understand ☐

The Blue Whale

Teacher Notes

Lesson Focus

Punctuation

- Capital letters for sentence beginnings
- Periods
- Exclamation marks
- Grammatical commas

Grammar

- Comparative/Superlative
- Collective nouns

Spelling

- Confused words: wail/whale, one/won, way/weigh, for/four, surface/service, breath/breathe
- Changing "y" to "i" to add suffixes "er" and "est"

Teacher Information

This descriptive report presents clear facts about the blue whale.

Answers

The largest animals ever to have been on the Earth are still living today**.**

The blue *whale* is much bigger than the largest dinosaurs**. One** blue whale measured nearly 112 feet and weighed more than 240 tons!

Everything about the blue whale is big**. E**ven its tongue may *weigh* up to *four* tons! **T**hey even call to each other in big voices which can be heard over 500 miles away**. T**hey are easily the loudest living creatures**.**

Because they are mammals⊙ blue whales breathe air**. T**his means they must come to the *surface* of the ocean to *breathe*. **T**he "waterspout" a whale blows out is not really water at all—it is hot *breath* and water vapor**.**

Mothers feed their young on milk**. B**y the time they are a year old⊙ the young calf may weigh more than 22 tons! **T**hey can live for up to 45 years**.**

1. (a) Missing punctuation is in **bold type**, commas are circled.
   (b) 2 commas
2. (a) Spelling errors are in *italic type*.
   whale, one, weigh, four, surface, breathe, breath
   (b) (i) funny, funnier, funniest
       (ii) sunny, sunnier, sunniest
3. (a) big, bigger, biggest
   loud, louder, loudest
   strange, stranger, strangest
   (b) a pod of whales
   a herd of cattle
   a flock of sheep
   a pride of lions

The Blue Whale

Editing

Read the report.

the largest animals ever to have been on the Earth are still living today

the blue (wail/whale) is much bigger than the largest dinosaurs (one/won) blue whale measured nearly 112 feet and weighed more than 240 tons

everything about the blue whale is big even its tongue may (way/weigh) up to (four/for) tons they also call to each other in big voices which can be heard over 500 miles away they are easily the loudest living creatures

because they are mammals, blue whales breathe air this means they must come to the (surface/service) of the ocean to (breath/breathe) the "waterspout" a whale blows out is not really water at all—it is hot (breathe/breath) and water vapor

mothers feed their young on milk by the time they are a year old, the young calf may weigh more than 22 tons they can live for up to 45 years

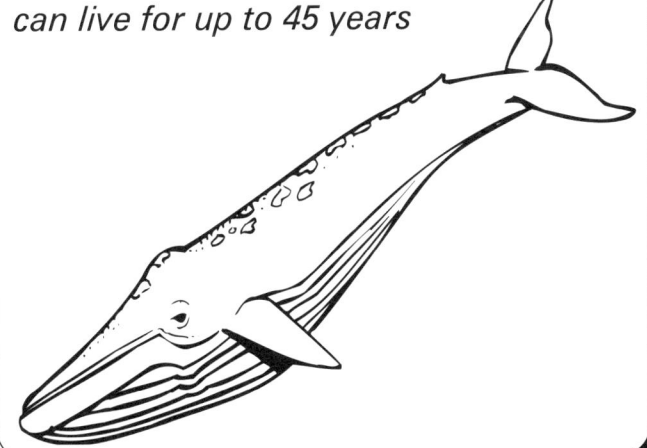

❶ Punctuation

(a) The report needs 13 capital letters, 10 periods and 3 exclamation marks. Circle the commas.

(b) How many commas are there? _____

❷ Spelling

(a) Circle the correct word in each bracket.

When changing words ending in "y," change the "y" to "i" and add the new ending; e.g., grumpy, grumpier, grumpiest.

(b) Make the -er and -est endings for the following adjectives.

(i) funny _____ _____

(ii) sunny _____ _____

❸ Grammar

When adjectives are used to compare different things, endings often change; e.g., large, larger, largest.

(a) Fill in the gaps in the table.

describes itself	compares with one other	compares with many others
big	bigger	
loud		loudest
strange		

Collective nouns are the names given to particular groups.

(b) Match each collective noun with the right animals.

a pod of • • whales
a herd of • • sheep
a flock of • • lions
a pride of • • cattle

Peep Loses Sheep

Teacher Notes

Lesson Focus

Punctuation

- Capital letters for sentence beginnings
- Capital letters for proper nouns
- Capital letters for the pronoun "I"
- Periods
- Exclamation marks
- Direct speech

Spelling

- Confused words: their/there, no/know, were/where, tails/tales
- Misspelled words

Grammar

- Contractions

Teacher Information

A recount is a retelling of past events in time order.

Answers

The disappearance of a flock of sheep *yesterday* has mystified both police and *their* owner.

Miss **P**eep, who was looking after her flock, said she *didn't* know *where* to find them.

"**I** *turned* my back for five minutes and they just vanished!" said a distressed **M**iss **P**eep. "I have been advised to *leave* them alone and they'll come home, but **I** just don't *know*!"

Anyone with *information* is asked to contact the police. **T**he sheep are easily distinguished by their wagging *tails*.

| yesterday |
| their |
| didn't |
| where |
| turned |
| leave |
| know |
| information |
| tails |

1. (a) Missing punctuation and punctuation to identify is in **bold type**.
   (b) (i) 4   (ii) 3
   (c) never
   (d) (i) Direct speech is underlined.
       (ii) Speech marks are circled.
   (e) (i) "Have you seen my sheep?" asked Bo Peep.
       (ii) "No I haven't," replied the farmer, "but I'll help you look for them."

2. (a) Spelling errors are in *italic type*.
   yesterday, their, didn't, where, turned, leave, know, information, tails

3. (a)

Contraction	1st Word	2nd Word
didn't	did	not
they'll	they	will
don't	do	not

   (b) (i) we're   (ii) couldn't
       (iii) I'd   (iv) won't

22   Editing - Book 2   © World Teachers Press® ~ www.worldteacherspress.com

Peep Loses Sheep

Editing

Read the recount.

the disappearance of a flock of sheep yesteday has _____
mystified both police and there owner _____

miss peep, who was looking after her flock, said she did'nt _____
know were to find them _____

"i terned my back for five minutes and they just vanished" _____
said a distressed miss peep "i have been advised to leaf _____
them alone and they'll come home, but i just don't no" _____

anyone with imformation is asked to contact the police _____
the sheep are easily distinguished by their wagging tales _____

❶ Punctuation

(a) The recount needs 10 capital letters, 5 periods and 2 exclamation marks.

(b) How many capital letters were used:

  (i) for proper nouns? _____

  (ii) for the word I? _____

(c) When is it correct to write the word "I" without a capital letter?

_____

(d) In the text:

  (i) highlight the words spoken by Bo Peep.

  (ii) circle the speech marks around these words.

(e) Add speech marks.

  (i) Have you seen my sheep? asked Bo Peep.

  (ii) No, I haven't, replied the farmer, but I'll help you look for them.

❷ Spelling

(a) Underline the spelling mistake on each line of text and write the correction at the end of the line.

❸ Grammar

(a) Write the three contractions used in the recount and the 2 words each is made from.

Contraction	1st Word	2nd Word

(b) Write these as contractions

  (i)   we are   _____

  (ii) could not   _____

  (iii) I would   _____

  (iv) will not   _____

Snake Bites

Teacher Notes

Lesson Focus

Punctuation
- Capital letters for sentence beginnings
- Periods
- Colons – recognition

Grammar
- Command verbs
- Common nouns
- Adjectives

Spelling
- Misspelled words

Vocabulary
- Synonyms

Teacher Information

A procedure shows how something is done. Instructions are written using command verbs, usually at the beginning of a sentence.

Answers

> **S**teps to follow if a person is bitten by a snake(:)
> 1. **C**heck for danger before helping the victim**.**
> 2. **B**e aware of the following *symptoms* or *sign*s(:)
>   - headache
>   - *sweating*
>   - nausea
>   - swelling
>   - *vomiting*
>   - double vision
>   - reddening of the affected area
>   - *pain* or tightness in the chest
> 3. **R**est and reassure the victim**.**
> 4. **A**pply a *pressure* bandage over the bitten area and around the limb**. I**f a bandage is unavailable, use strips of material**.**
> 5. **S**eek medical aid immediately**.**
>   **S**ymptoms can occur 15 minutes to two hours after the bite**.**

1. (a) Missing punctuation and punctuation to identify is in **bold type**, colons are circled.
2. (a) Spelling errors are in *italic type*.
   symptoms, signs, sweating, pain, pressure, limb
3. (a) Students choose six of the following: Check, Be aware, Rest, reassure, Apply, use, Seek
   (b) See underlined words:
   chest, limb, person, victim
   (c) (i) double vision (ii) affected/bitten area
   (iii) pressure bandage (iv) medical aid
4. (a) Teacher check

Snake Bites

Editing

> **Read the procedure.**
>
> steps to follow if a person is bitten by a snake:
> 1. check for danger before helping the victim
> 2. be aware of the following simtoms or sines:
>   - headache
>   - swetting
>   - nausea
>   - swelling
>   - vomiting
>   - double vision
>   - reddening of the affected area
>   - payne or tightness in the chest
> 3. rest and reassure the victim
> 4. apply a preshu bandage over the bitten area and around the lim if a bandage is unavailable, use strips of material
> 5. seek medical aid immediately
>
> **symptoms can occur 15 minutes to two hours after the bite**

❶ Punctuation
(a) The procedure needs 8 capital letters at the beginning of sentences and 6 periods. Circle the colons used to show things in a list.

❷ Spelling
(a) Six words are misspelled. Underline, then write the correct spelling.

_____   _____

_____   _____

_____   _____

❸ Grammar
Procedures use command verbs which tell what to do.

(a) Write 6 command verbs from the text.

_____   _____

_____   _____

_____   _____

(b) Circle 2 nouns (naming words) to do with the body and 2 "people" nouns.

(c) Write adjectives (describing words) from the text to match the nouns.

(i) _____ vision

(ii) _____ area

(iii) _____ bandage

(iv) _____ aid

❹ Vocabulary
Synonyms are words which have nearly the same meaning as another word.

(a) Write synonyms for:

(i) aid _____

(ii) symptom _____

(iii) area _____

(iv) seek _____

Chocolate

Teacher Notes

Lesson Focus

Punctuation

- Capital letter at the beginning of each line of a poem
- Commas in a list

Grammar

- Adverbs
- Adjectives

Spelling

- Misspelled words

Writing

- Sentences

Teacher Information

The descriptive poem on the student page is a cinquain. A cinquain is a five-line poem that describes something and follows this pattern:

Line 1 consists of one word or two syllables to describe the topic.
Line 2 consists of two words or four syllables to describe the title.
Line 3 consists of three words or six syllables to describe what the topic does.
Line 4 consists of four words or eight syllables to describe the mood or feeling.
Line 5 consists of one word or two syllables with a similar meaning to the topic.

Answers

Chocolate	Chocolate
Soft**,** *smooth*	smooth
Melts on the *tongue* slowly	tongue
Comforting**,** soothing and *delightful*	delightful
Chocolate	Chocolate

1. Missing punctuation is in **bold type**.
2. (a) Spelling errors are in *italic type*.
   chocolate, smooth, tongue, delightful, chocolate
3. (a) slowly
   (b) (i) quickly   (ii) softly
       (iii) smoothly   (iv) sweetly
       (v) loudly   (vi) firmly
       (vii) beautifully (viii) swiftly
   (c) Possible answers: soft, smooth, comforting, soothing, delightful
   (d) Teacher check
4. (a) Teacher check

Chocolate

Read the poem.

choclat

soft smoothe

melts on the tung slowly

comforting soothing and deliteful

choclat

❶ Punctuation

(a) The cinquain poem needs 5 capital letters at the beginning of the lines.

Commas are usually placed between a list of words in a sentence.

(b) Put in the 2 commas missing in the poem.

❷ Spelling

(a) Underline the spelling mistake on each line of text and write the correction at the end of the line.

❸ Grammar

Adverbs add descriptions to verbs. Often they end in "-ly."

(a) Write the adverb in the poem.

_____

(b) Add -ly to these words to make adverbs:

(i) quick_____   (ii) soft_____

(iii) smooth_____   (iv) sweet_____

(v) loud_____   (vi) firm_____

(vii) beautiful_____   (viii) swift_____

Adjectives are words which describe a noun.

(c) Write 4 adjectives used in the poem.

_____ _____

_____ _____

(d) Write 3 different adjectives you would use to describe chocolate.

_____

_____

_____

❹ Writing

(a) Rewrite the text in sentences, using the original words.

_____

_____

_____

_____

_____

_____

_____

The Wind and the Sun

Teacher Notes

Lesson Focus

Punctuation

- Capital letters for sentence beginnings
- Capital letter for the pronoun "I"
- Periods
- Grammatical commas
- Direct speech

Grammar

- Adverbs

Spelling

- Confused words: sun/son, you/ewe, blew/blue, might/mite, wrapped/rapt
- Misspelled words

Vocabulary

- Synonyms

Teacher Information

This narrative, in the form of a fable, describes a series of events in time order, involving fictitious characters.

Answers

The wind and the *sun* were having an argument**.**

"**I**'m stronger than *you*," announced the wind aggressively**.**

"**N**o, **I**'m stronger than you," replied the sun *calmly*.

They agreed to have a contest to solve the argument**.**

A man was walking in the distance, *wrapped* in a thick, winter coat. **T**he sun suggested that whoever could make him remove his coat would be the winner of the contest**. T**he wind agreed to this idea and chose to try first**.**

He *blew* with all his *might,* but the man held on to his coat more tightly than ever**.**

The sun smiled**. H**e began to shine, gently at first, then more strongly. **T**he man undid his coat as the sun continued to *beam***. A**t last, he took it off**.**

The moral of this fable is, the art of persuasion is greater than the strength of force.

1. (a) Missing punctuation is in **bold type**, commas are circled.
   (b) 9 commas
   (c) Direct speech is underlined.
2. (a) Spelling errors are in *italic type*. sun, you, calmly, wrapped, blew, might, beam
3. (a) (i) announced – aggressively
       (ii) replied – calmly
       (iii) held on – tightly
   (b) Teacher check
4. (a) announced, replied, suggested

The Wind and the Sun

Editing

Read the fable.

the wind and the (sun/son) were having an argument

"i'm stronger than (ewe/you)," announced the wind aggressively

"no, i'm stronger than you," replied the sun (calmly/carmly)

they agreed to have a contest to solve the argument

a man was walking in the distance, (wrapped/rapt) in a thick winter coat the sun suggested that whoever could make him remove his coat would be the winner of the contest the wind agreed to this idea and chose to try first

he (blue/blew) with all his (mite/might), but the man held on to his coat more tightly than ever

the sun smiled he began to shine, gently at first, then more strongly the man undid his coat as the sun continued to (beam/beem) at last, he took it off

the moral of this fable is, the art of persuasion is greater than the strength of force

❶ Punctuation

(a) The narrative needs 14 capital letters and 13 periods. Circle the commas.

(b) How many commas are there? _____

Speech marks are put at the beginning and end of what is said by each person in a conversation.

(c) Find the speech marks and underline the words spoken by the wind and the sun.

❷ Spelling

(a) Circle the correct word in each bracket.

❸ Grammar

An adverb describes a verb.

(a) Write the adverb used in the text to describe these verbs.

  (i) announced _____

  (ii) replied _____

  (iii) held on _____

(b) Choose an adverb to go with each of these verbs.

  (i) He growled _____

  (ii) We ate _____

  (iii) I shivered _____

  (iv) They laughed _____

❹ Vocabulary

Synonyms are words with similar meanings which can be used in a piece of text to make it more interesting. The word "said" is often overused in writing.

(a) In the text, underline the 3 words which have been used instead of "said."

Coconut Cookies

Teacher Notes

Lesson Focus

Punctuation
- Capital letters for sentence beginnings
- Periods

Grammar
- Command verbs

Spelling
- Confused words: flour/flower, plain/plane, roll/role, to/too/two

Writing
- Sentences

Teacher Information

A procedure explains how something is made or done. Instructions are written using command verbs, usually at the beginning of a sentence.

Answers

Ingredients:
- 1 cup shredded coconut
- 1/2 tsp bicarbonate of soda
- 1 cup plain flour
- 1 cup rolled oats
- 1/4 cup light karo
- 1 tbsp boiling water
- 2/3 cup sugar
- 1 stick butter

Equipment:
- cookie sheet
- large mixing bowl
- flour sifter
- parchment paper
- small saucepan
- spoons

Steps:
- **H**eat oven to 350°.
- **L**ine cookie sheet with parchment paper.
- **S**ift flour and sugar into large bowl.
- **A**dd oats and coconut.
- **M**ake a well in the center of the mixture.
- **C**ombine butter and syrup in saucepan.
- **S**tir over low heat.
- **R**emove from heat.
- **D**issolve bicarbonate of soda in water.
- **A**dd to butter mixture.
- **A**dd butter mixture to dry ingredients.
- **M**ix to combine.
- **R**oll one level tablespoon of mixture into a ball and repeat until all mixture is used.
- **F**latten balls slightly on tray.
- **A**llow room for spreading.
- **B**ake 20 minutes until just brown.

1. (a) Missing punctuation is in **bold type**.
2. (a) (i) flower
   (ii) plane
   (iii) role
   (iv) too, two
3. (a) Heat, Line, Sift, Add, Make, Combine, Stir, Remove, Dissolve, Add, Add, Mix, Roll, repeat, Flatten, Allow, Bake
4. (a) (i) Heat oven to 350°.
   (ii) Stir over low heat.

Coconut Cookies

Editing

Read the procedure.

Ingredients:
- 1 cup shredded coconut
- ¼ cup light karo
- ½ tsp bicarbonate of soda
- 1 tbsp boiling water
- 1 cup plain flour
- 1 cup rolled oats
- ⅔ cup sugar
- 1 stick butter

Equipment:
- cookie sheet
- large mixing bowl
- flour sifter
- parchment paper
- small saucepan
- spoons

Steps:
- heat oven to 350°
- line cookie sheet with parchment paper
- sift flour and sugar into large bowl
- add oats and coconut
- make a well in the center of the mixture
- combine butter and syrup in saucepan
- stir over low heat
- remove from heat
- dissolve bicarbonate of soda in water
- add to butter mixture
- add butter mixture to dry ingredients
- mix to combine
- roll one level tablespoon of mixture into a ball and repeat until all mixture is used
- flatten balls slightly on tray
- allow room for spreading
- bake 20 minutes until just brown

❶ *Punctuation*

(a) The procedure needs 16 capital letters and periods.

❷ *Spelling*

Homophones are words which have different meanings and spelling but sound the same.

(a) Find homophones of these words.

(i) flour _____

(ii) plain _____

(iii) roll _____

(iv) to _____

❸ *Grammar*

(a) Find and underline all the command verbs.

❹ *Writing*

Procedures need to give clear, concise instructions.

(a) Rewrite each instruction, leaving out all the unnecessary words, so it is the same as one of the steps in the procedure.

(i) *Turn on the oven and heat it up so that it reaches 350°.*

_____

(ii) *Turn the gas on to low and put the saucepan on it. Then get the spoon and place it in the saucepan and stir the mixture.*

_____

Alaskan Vacation

Teacher Notes

Lesson Focus

Punctuation

- Capital letters for sentence beginnings
- Capital letters for proper nouns
- Periods
- Commas in lists
- Apostrophes for contractions

Grammar

- Verbs–past tense
- Contractions

Spelling

- Confused words: to/two/too, hour/our, through/threw, bored/board, wear/where, hole/whole, of/off, write/right, your/you're
- Misspelled words

Writing

- Paragraphs

Teacher Information

A recount is a retelling of past events in time order.

Answers

> **D**ear **C**arol**,**
>
> **M**y *vacation to* **A**laska was fantastic**.** **I**'ll tell you about it**.**
>
> **A**fter the long flight from **A**ustralia**,** we landed in **V**ancouver, where a bus transferred us to *our* cruise ship**.** **I**t took ages to get *through* customs and immigration, but finally we were on *board*. **W**e explored the ship and found the pools**,** restaurants**,** the gym and places *where* you could get free hamburgers**,** hot dogs**,** pizza and ice cream**.**
>
> **W**e visited an interesting port every *second* day**.** **W**e anchored next to a glacier for a *whole* day and watched the ice breaking *off*. **I**t was really loud**.**
>
> **P**lease *write* and tell me about your holiday**.**
>
> **Y**our friend, **J**ill

1. (a) Missing punctuation is in **bold type**.
   (b) I'll
   (c) I and will
   (d) Carol, Alaska, Australia, Vancouver, Jill
2. (a) Spelling errors are in *italic type*.
   holiday, to, our, through, board, where, second, whole, off, write, Your
3. (a) Answers will include: was, landed, transferred, took, were, explored, found, visited, anchored, watched
   (b) (i) told   (ii) wrote
   (c) (i) she, will   (ii) did, not
       (iii) I, would or I, had   (iv) do, not
4. (a) Paragraph 3

32 Editing - Book 2   © World Teachers Press® ~ www.worldteacherspress.com

Alaskan Vacation

Editing

Read the recount.

dear carol,

my (vakation/vacation) (two/too/to) alaska was fantastic i'll tell you about it

after the long flight from australia, we landed in vancouver where a bus transferred us to (hour/our) cruise ship it took ages to get (threw/through) customs and immigration, but finally we were on (board/bored) we explored the ship and found the pools restaurants the gym and places (wear/where) you could get free hamburgers hot dogs pizza and ice-cream

we visited an interesting port every (second/sekond) day we anchored next to a glacier for a (hole/whole) day and watched the ice breaking (off/of) it was really loud

please (write/right) and tell me about your holiday

(your/you're) friend, jill

❶ Punctuation

(a) The recount needs 16 capital letters, 9 periods and 4 commas (in lists).

(b) Which contraction is used in

the letter? _____

(c) What is it a contraction of?

_____ and _____

Proper nouns need capital letters.

(d) Write the 5 proper nouns used in the recount.

_____

_____

_____

❷ Spelling

(a) Circle the correct word in each bracket.

❸ Grammar

Recounts are usually written in the past tense.

(a) Circle any 6 past tense verbs.

(b) Change these 2 present tense verbs into the past tense.

  (i) tell _____ (ii) write _____

(c) Write the 2 words used in each of these contractions.

  (i) she'll _____ and _____

  (ii) didn't _____ and _____

  (iii) I'd _____ and _____

  (iv) don't _____ and _____

❹ Writing

There are 4 paragraphs in the letter.

(a) Which paragraph describes the places the ship visited? _____

Pet Parade

Teacher Notes

Lesson Focus

Punctuation
- Capital letters for sentence beginnings
- Periods
- Question marks
- Exclamation marks
- Direct speech

Grammar
- Adjectives
- Contractions

Spelling
- Confused words: would/wood, heard/herd, where/wear
- Misspelled words

Vocabulary
- Synonyms
- Antonyms

Teacher Information

This narrative tells a story in a sequence of events involving fictional characters.

Answers

"**I**t's time for the pet parade," Mrs. Sindle said to her class. "**I**f your pet is still outside, you had better bring it into the classroom now."

Phillip put up his hand**.**

"**Y**es, Phillip, what's *wrong***?**"

"Mrs. Sindle, I think I'd better leave my pet outside**. H**e *would* fight all the other pets—and probably eat them, too."

"**H**eavens**! W**hat sort of pet is it, Phillip**?**"

"**I**t's a long-nosed, long-tailed, short-legged, hairless terrier," said Phillip, very proudly**.**

"**I** don't think I've ever *heard* of that animal *before*," said Mrs. Sindle**. "D**oes it have another name**?**"

"**O**h, yes, Mrs. Sindle**. I**n Africa, *where* it comes from, they call it a crocodile**!**"

1. (a) Missing punctuation is in **bold type**.
   (b) Direct speech is underlined.
2. (a) Spelling errors are in *italic type*.
   wrong, would, heard, before, where
3. (a) (i) I'd (ii) it's
       (iii) don't (iv) I've
       (v) what's
   (b) long-nosed, long-tailed, short-legged, hairless
4. (a) Teacher check
   (b) (i) outside
       (ii) comes
       (iii) before

34   Editing - Book 2   © World Teachers Press® ~ www.worldteacherspress.com

Pet Parade

Editing

Read the narrative.

"it's time for the pet parade," Mrs. Sindle said to her class "if your pet is still outside, you had better bring it into the classroom now"

Phillip put up his hand

"yes, Phillip, what's (rong/wrong)"

"Mrs. Sindle, I think I'd better leave my pet outside he (wood/would) fight all the other pets—and probably eat them, too"

"Heavens what sort of pet is it, Phillip"

"it's a long-nosed, long-tailed, short-legged, hairless terrier," said Phillip, very proudly

"i don't think I've ever (heard/herd) of that animal (befour/before)," said Mrs. Sindle "does it have another name"

"oh, yes, Mrs. Sindle in Africa, (where/wear) it comes from, they call it a crocodile"

❶ Punctuation

(a) The narrative needs 11 capital letters for the beginning of sentences, 8 periods, 3 question marks and 2 exclamation marks.

Speech marks are put at the beginning and end of what is said by each person in a conversation.

(b) Using a different color for each person, underline the words spoken by Mrs. Sindle and Phillip.

❷ Spelling

(a) Circle the correct word in each bracket.

❸ Grammar

An apostrophe is used in place of missing letters in contractions

(a) Find the 5 contractions in the text and write them after the two words.

(i) I had _____   (ii) it is _____

(iii) do not _____   (iv) I have _____

(v) what is _____

(b) Write the adjectives Phillip uses to describe his pet.

_____

_____

❹ Vocabulary

(a) Choose a better word to replace the word "said" each time it appears in the text.

_____   _____

_____

(b) Find words used in the text with the opposite meaning to these words.

(i) inside _____

(ii) goes _____

(iii) after _____

The Gecko

Teacher Notes

Lesson Focus

Punctuation
- Capital letters for sentence beginnings
- Periods

Spelling
- Misspelled words

Grammar
- Adjectives
- Contractions

Vocabulary
- Compound words

Teacher Information

Descriptions describe the characteristics, components or functions of specific living or non-living things.

Answers

A gecko is a *type* of lizard. **G**eckos are found all around the world. **G**eckos are *different* from other lizards. **T**hey have large pads on their feet. **T**hese pads help them to hold on when *climbing*. **T**hey have large eyes *which* do not have eyelids. **T**hey can use their *tongues* to lick their eyes clean. **T**heir *bodies* are covered in soft skin with tiny scales. **S**ome are as small as 2 inches and others grow up to 1 foot in *length*. **G**eckos are nocturnal and like to feed on *insects*.

type
different
They
climbing
which
tongues
bodies
Some
length
insects

1. (a) Missing punctuation is in **bold type**.
2. (a) Spelling errors are in *italic type*.
   type, different, they, climbing, which, tongues, bodies, some, length, insects
3. (a) (i) large   (ii) large   (iii) soft   (iv) tiny
   (b) different, nocturnal
   (c) (i) don't   (ii) they've
4. (a) Answers include: eyeball, eyebrow, eyelash, eyesight, eyesore, eyetooth, eyewitness

The Gecko

Editing

Read the description.

a gecko is a tipe of lizard geckos are found all
around the world geckos are diffrent from other
lizards thay have large pads on their feet these
pads help them to hold on when climing they
have large eyes witch do not have eyelids they
can use their tungs to lick their eyes clean their
bodys are covered in soft skin with tiny scales
sum are as small as 2 inches and others grow up to
1 foot in lenth geckos are nocturnal and
like to feed on insecs

_____
_____
_____
_____
_____
_____
_____
_____
_____
_____

❶ Punctuation

(a) The description needs 10 missing capital letters and 10 periods.

❷ Spelling

(a) Underline the spelling mistake on each line of text and write the correction at the end of the line.

❸ Grammar

An adjective describes a noun.

(a) Write adjectives from the text to match these nouns:

(i) _____ pads

(ii) _____ eyes

(iii) _____ skin

(iv) _____ scales

(b) Circle 2 other words which describe geckos.

Contractions are words made by joining two words and shortening them by taking out letters and adding an apostrophe.

(c) Write the contraction for:

(i) do not _____

(ii) they have _____

❹ Vocabulary

Compound words are smaller words joined to make larger words. "Eyelid" is made by joining the words "eye" and "lid" together.

(a) In the box below, write compound words that start with "eye."

Fish for Classroom Pets

Teacher Notes

Lesson Focus

Punctuation

- Capital letters for sentence beginnings
- Capital letters for proper nouns
- Periods
- Commas in lists
- Grammatical commas

Grammar

- Present tense verbs
- Contractions

Spelling

- Confused words: chose/choose, they're/there/their, for/from, weak/week, by/buy, wear/where, would/wood, of/off
- Misspelled words

Vocabulary

- Compound words

Teacher Information

Expositions are written or spoken to persuade others to think or do something.

Answers

Mrs. **H**unter**,** girls and boys**,** I believe that we must *choose* fish as our *class* pets**.**	choose
	class
Fish are beautiful and very relaxing to watch**.** *They're* silent and they won't stop us *from* hearing **M**rs. **H**unter or *each* other**.**	they're
	from
	each
Fish are easy to look after**.** **W**e *would* only need to clean their tank every few *weeks* and to remember to feed them once a day**.** **T**he weekends *wouldn't* be a problem**.** **T**hey could stay in the classroom and we could *buy* some *of* that slow-release fish food**.**	would
	weeks
	wouldn't
	buy
	of
Another good argument is cost**.** I know *where* we can borrow a tank and a pump**.** **W**e'd only need to *buy* the fish and a little bit of fish food**.** **T**hey *don't* eat much**.** *P*lease support me by voting FISH 1 in our class pet ballot**.**	where
	buy
	don't
	Please

1. Missing punctuation is **bold type**.
2. (a) Spelling errors are in *italic type*.
   choose, class, they're, from, each, would, weeks, wouldn't, buy, of, where, buy, don't, please
3. (a) Answers will include: believe, choose, are, need, be, stay, buy, is, know, can borrow, eat, support
   (b) Answers will include:
   they're – they are
   won't – will not
   wouldn't – would not
   we'd – we would
   don't – do not
4. (a) weekends, classroom
   (b) Teacher check

Fish for Classroom Pets

Editing

Read the exposition.

mrs. hunter girls and boys I believe that we must chose _____

fish as our classe pets _____

fish are beautiful and very relaxing to watch there _____

silent and they won't stop us for hearing mrs. hunter _____

or eech other _____

fish are easy to look after we wood only need to clean _____

their tank every few weaks and to remember to feed _____

them once a day the weekends woodn't be a problem _____

they could stay in the classroom and we could by some _____

off that slow-release fish food _____

another good argument is cost i know wear we can _____

borrow a tank and a pump we'd only need to by the _____

fish and a little bit of fish food they do'nt eat much _____

pleese support me by voting FISH 1 in our class pet ballot _____

❶ Punctuation

(a) The exposition needs 12 capital letters for sentence beginnings, 3 more for proper nouns and 12 periods.

(b) Add 2 commas in the first line.

❷ Spelling

(a) Find the misspelled word in each line and write it correctly at the end of the line.

❸ Grammar

Expositions are usually written in the present tense.

(a) Write any 2 present tense verbs from the text.

_____ _____

(b) (i) Underline 3 contractions.

(ii) List the contractions with the two words they are made from.

contraction	word	word

❹ Vocabulary

(a) Circle 2 compound words.

(b) Write a compound word using:

(i) room _____

(ii) side _____

The Egg and Bottle Experiment

Teacher Notes

Lesson Focus

Punctuation

- Capital letters for sentence beginnings
- Periods
- Grammatical commas
- Exclamation marks
- Colons – recognition

Spelling

- Misspelled words

Grammar

- Command verbs
- Comparative and superlative

Teacher Information

A procedure outlines how something is done.
An explanation outlines how something works or is made.

Answers

You will need**:**

- a hard-boiled egg without the shell
- a bottle with a neck slightly smaller *than* the egg
- a *piece* of paper
- a match

Method**:**

1. **C**heck that the egg will sit firmly in the neck of the bottle**.**
2. **T**ear the paper into *strips* and put them into the bottle**.**
3. **L**ight the paper by dropping a *burning* match into the bottle**.**
4. **Q**uickly set the egg in the neck of the bottle**. Y**ou will see the egg being sucked into the bottle with a gurgle and a pop**!**

How it works:

As the paper *burns***,** it uses up all the oxygen in the air**. T**he egg has sealed the neck of the bottle so no more air can get inside**. T**his reduces the air pressure inside the *bottle* and the egg is sucked in**. I**n fact**,** the outside air *pressure* pushes the egg into the bottle**!**

1. (a)–(b) Missing punctuation is in **bold type**.
   (c) Colons are circled.
2. (a) Spelling errors are in *italic type*.
   than, piece, check, strips, burning, burns, bottle, pressure
3. (a) Check, Tear, put, Light, set
   (b) tall, taller, tallest
   quick, quicker, quickest
   high, higher, highest

The Egg and Bottle Experiment

Editing

Read the procedure and explanation.

You will need:
- a hard-boiled egg without the shell
- a bottle with a neck slightly smaller then the egg
- a peice of paper
- a match

Method:
1. chek that the egg will sit firmly in the neck of the bottle
2. tear the paper into stripes and put them into the bottle
3. light the paper by dropping a berning match into the bottle
4. quickly set the egg in the neck of the bottle you will see the egg being sucked into the bottle with a gurgle and a pop

How it works:

as the paper berns it uses up all the oxygen in the air the egg has sealed the neck of the bottle so no more air can get inside this reduces the air pressure inside the bottel and the egg is sucked in in fact the outside air pressa pushes the egg into the bottle

❶ *Punctuation*

(a) Find 9 missing capital letters, 7 periods, and 2 exclamation marks.

(b) 2 commas are missing from the "How it works" section.

(c) Circle the 2 colons used to show things in a list.

❷ *Spelling*

(a) 8 words are misspelled. Underline them, then write the correct spelling.

_____ _____

_____ _____

_____ _____

_____ _____

❸ *Grammar*

Command verbs are used in procedures to tell you what to do.

(a) Write the 5 command verbs from the "Method" section.

_____ _____

_____ _____

_____

When we use adjectives to compare different things, the ending of the adjective often changes; e.g., small, smaller, smallest.

(b) Fill in the gaps in the table.

describes itself	compares with one other	compares with many others
tall	taller	
quick		quickest
high		

Explorer's Diary

Teacher Notes

Lesson Focus

Punctuation

- Capital letters for sentence beginnings
- Capital letters for proper nouns
- Periods
- Exclamation marks
- Grammatical commas

Grammar

- Verb tenses
- Pronouns

Spelling

- Confused words: two/to/too, threw/through/though, hear/here, buy/by
- Misspelled words

Vocabulary

- Shortened forms

Teacher Information

A diary is a recount of a past event.

Answers

Sunday **M**arch 14

This morning we left the river and *traveled* inland**.** **W**e made our way through the razor sharp twigs and *brambles* and arrived at a clearing at dusk**.** **W**e made camp here**.**

Tuesday **M**arch 16

We left camp yesterday with 8 natives**.** **W**e spent *two* days trying to get *through* the jungle to the river ... by sunset we could *hear* the splash of a *waterfall***.**

Wednesday **M**arch 17

At sunlight**,** we left camp and followed the sound of the waterfall**.** **T**here it was**!** **W**e had found the famous circular lake**.** **W**e slept *by* the lake with the native *guides***.**

1. (a) Missing punctuation is in **bold type**.
2. Spelling errors are in *italic type*.
   - (a) two, through, hear, by
   - (b) traveled, brambles, waterfall, guides
3. (a) 9
   - (b) (i) will leave (ii) will arrive (iii) will spend (iv) will follow
4. (a) (i) February (ii) centimeter(s) (iii) United States of America

Explorer's Diary

Editing

Read this recount in the form of a diary.

sunday march 14

this morning we left the river and traveld inland we made our way through the razor sharp twigs and brambls and arrived at a clearing at dusk we made camp here

tuesday march 16

we left camp yesterday with 8 natives we spent (too/two/to) days trying to get (threw/through/though) the jungle to the river ... by sunset we could (hear/here) the splash of a wortufall

wednesday march 17

at sunlight we left camp and followed the sound of the waterfall there it was we had found the famous circular lake we slept (by/buy) the lake with the native gides

❶ Punctuation

(a) The recount needs 9 capital letters at the beginning of sentences, 6 capital letters for proper nouns, 8 periods, 1 exclamation mark and 1 comma in the last entry.

❷ Spelling

(a) Circle the correct word in each bracket.

(b) Four different words are misspelled. Write the correct spelling.

_____ _____

_____ _____

❸ Grammar

Pronouns may be used in place of a noun. In the text, "it" is used to mean the circular lake.

(a) The pronoun "we" is used _____ times in the text.

Verbs in the future tense often use the word "will."

(b) Change these verbs from past tense to future tense:

(i) left _____

(ii) arrived _____

(iii) spent _____

(iv) followed _____

❹ Vocabulary

Shortened forms can be used for words and for groups of words; e.g., Sun. (Sunday), PO (Post Office), kg (kilograms).

(a) Write these in full.

(i) Feb. _____

(ii) cm _____

(iii) USA _____

The Beach

Teacher Notes

Lesson Focus

Punctuation
- Capital letters for sentence beginnings
- Periods
- Commas in a list
- Grammatical commas

Grammar
- Adjectives

Writing
- Sentences

Spelling
- Confused words: clothe/cloth, son/sun, shore/sure
- Misspelled words

Vocabulary
- Similes

Teacher Information

This description of a beach describes its physical characteristics.

Answers

> **G**lorious, white sand covered the ground <u>like a jewel-studded *carpet*</u>. **T**he hot sun, slowly *moving* toward the horizon, caused each grain to sparkle <u>like a diamond</u>. **T**he ocean lay <u>like a vast expanse of shiny, turquoise *cloth*</u>, glittering in the early evening *sun*. **T**he surf was active but not *angry*. **T**he next breaker rose <u>like a curved wall</u> as it traveled *towards* the *shore*.

1. (a) Missing punctuation and punctuation to identify is in **bold type**.
   (b) The 5 commas are circled.
2. Spelling errors are in *italic type*.
   (a) cloth, sun, shore
   (b) carpet, moving, angry, toward
3. (a) (i) glorious, white (ii) glittering (iii) active, (not) angry
   (iv) curved (v) early
4. (a) Similes are <u>underlined</u>
   … like a jewel-studded carpet.
   … like a diamond.
   … like a vast expanse of shiny, turquoise cloth.
   … like a curved wall.
5. (a) Teacher check

The Beach

Editing

Read the description.

glorious, white sand covered the ground like a jewel-studded carpit the hot sun, slowly moveing toward the horizon, caused each grain to sparkle like a diamond the ocean lay like a vast expanse of shiny, turquoise (clothe/cloth), glittering in the early evening (son/sun) the surf was active but not angre the next breaker rose like a curved wall as it traveled tooward the (shore/sure)

❶ Punctuation

(a) The description needs 5 capital letters and 5 periods.

(b) Circle all the commas. How many are there? _____

❷ Spelling

(a) Circle the correct word in each bracket.

(b) Write the correct spelling of the 4 misspelled words.

_____ _____

_____ _____

❸ Grammar

Adjectives are used to describe nouns.

(a) Write the adjectives used to describe these nouns in the text.

   (i) the sand _____

   (ii) the ocean _____

   (iii) the surf _____

   (iv) a wall _____

   (v) the evening _____

❹ Vocabulary

*A simile compares one thing with another; e.g., He ran **like** the wind; **as** blind as a bat.*

(a) Underline, then write the 4 similes in the text.

• _____

• _____

• _____

• _____

❺ Writing

Our sense of smell is very powerful in reminding us of a particular place.

(a) Using adjectives and similes, write a sentence to describe the smell of a place you know.

_____

_____

Elephants Can Fly!

Teacher Notes

Lesson Focus

Punctuation
- Capital letters for sentence beginnings
- Capital letters for proper nouns
- Periods
- Grammatical commas
- Apostrophes for possession

Grammar
- Apostrophes for possession
- Verb tense – present, past, future

Spelling
- Confused words: two/too/to, male/mail, which/witch, flew/flu
- Misspelled words

Writing
- Paragraphs

Teacher Information

A recount is a retelling of events in time order.

Answers

> **T**his morning, **L**ondon's **H**eathrow **A**irport was the center of a massive operation. **Two** fully grown **I**ndian elephants were flown in from **M**umbai, **I**ndia, as part of a worldwide breeding program.
>
> **T**he elephants, a young female named **T**risha and **R**ajah, a ten-year-old *male*, will be housed in specially constructed compounds at the **L**ondon **Z**oo. **T**hey will join **M**isha, a long-time resident and a favorite with the zoo's *many* visitors.
>
> **M**artin **J**ones, the coordinator of the ambitious project, told reporters that the elephants, *which* traveled in specially designed crates, *flew* very well.

1. (a) Missing punctuation and punctuation to identify is in **bold type**.
   (b) The 11 commas are circled.
   (c) Words with apostrophes are underlined.
       London's, zoo's
   (d) To show ownership
2. (a) Spelling errors are in *italic type*.
       two, male, many, which, flew
3. (a) (i) the elephants' tails   (ii) the children's visit   (iii) Trisha's compound
   (b) past tense: was, were flown, told, traveled, flew
       future tense: will be housed, will join
   (c) the past tense
4. (a) 3
   (b) Teacher check. Paragraph 1 explains what happened at Heathrow Airport.

Elephants Can Fly!

Editing

Read the recount.

this morning, london's heathrow airport <u>was</u> the centre of a massive operation (two/too) fully grown indian elephants <u>were</u> <u>flown</u> in from mumbai, india as part of a worldwide breeding program

the elephants, a young female named trisha and rajah, a ten-year-old (mail/male), <u>will be housed</u> in specially constructed compounds at the london zoo they <u>will join</u> misha, a long-time resident and a favorite with the zoo's (many/meny) visitors

martin jones, the coordinator of the ambitious project, <u>told</u> reporters that the elephants, (which/witch) <u>traveled</u> in specially designed crates, (flu/flew) very well

❶ Punctuation

(a) The recount needs 17 capital letters (13 for proper nouns) and 5 periods.

(b) Circle all the commas. How many are there? _____

(c) Circle the words with apostrophes.

(d) Why is there an apostrophe in these two words?

_____

_____

❷ Spelling

(a) Highlight the correct spelling of the words in brackets.

❸ Grammar

An apostrophe is used to show ownership. It goes after the owner(s); e.g., the lady's bag, the ladies' bags.

(a) Add apostrophes to show ownership.

   (i)   the elephants tails

   (ii) the childrens visit

   (iii) Trishas compound

(b) There are 7 verbs underlined in the text. Write each verb in the correct column according to its tense.

Past tense	Future tense

(c) Which tense was more often used?

_____

❹ Writing

(a) How many paragraphs are there in this recount? _____

(b) What does the first paragraph explain?

_____

_____

_____

How a Thermometer Works

Teacher Notes

Lesson Focus

Punctuation

- Capital letters for sentence beginnings
- Periods
- Commas in a list

Grammar

- Indefinite articles, "a" or "an"
- Plural nouns

Spelling

- Confused words: an/a, roll/role, maid/made, which/witch
- Misspelled words

Teacher Information

An explanation analyzes how something works, is made, or how or why things happen.

Answers

A thermometer is *an* instrument used to measure heat**.**	an
Thermometers are *made* from a glass tube with a scale on the outside and filled with a liquid, *usually* mercury**.**	made
	usually
Mercury is the liquid which is most *often* used because it always changes in the same way when the same *temperature* is applied**.** **I**t fills a glass bulb, *which* is connected to a thin sealed tube, also partially *filled* with mercury**.** **W**hen the glass tube is warmed, the mercury expands and rises to the same *point* in the tube whenever the same *amount* of heat is applied**.**	often
	temperature
	which
	filled
	point
	amount
Thermometers are used for *many* purposes, including medicine**,** science and in cooking**.** **T**hey play *an* important *role* in our lives**.**	many
	an
	role

1. (a) Missing punctuation is in **bold type**.
2. (a) Spelling errors are in *italic type*.
   an, made, usually, often, temperature, which, filled, point, amount, many, an, role
3. (a) Plural nouns are underlined.
   Thermometers, purposes, lives
   (b) a: thermometer, glass, scale, liquid, thin
   an: instrument, important
   (c) Teacher check. It is difficult to say two consecutive vowel sounds.

How a Thermometer Works

Read the explanation.

Editing

a thermometer is a instrument used to measure heat　_____

thermometers are maid from a glass tube with a scale　_____

on the outside, and filled with a liquid, usualy mercury　_____

mercury is the liquid which is most ofen used because it　_____

always changes in the same way when the same tempature　_____

is applied it fills a glass bulb, wich is connected to a thin sealed　_____

tube, also partially filed with mercury when the glass tube is　_____

warmed, the mercury expands and rises to the same piont in　_____

the tube whenever the same amownt of heat is applied　_____

thermometers are used for meny purposes, including　_____

medicine science and in cooking they play a important　_____

roll in our lives　_____

❶ Punctuation

(a) The explanation needs 7 capital letters, 7 periods and 1 comma in the last paragraph.

❷ Spelling

(a) Underline the spelling mistake on each line of text and write the correction at the end of the line.

❸ Grammar

(a) Write the 3 plural nouns used in the text.

_____

_____

_____

(b) Underline all the words following "a" and "an" in the text. List them below.

words following "a"	words following "an"

(c) Explain why it is sometimes necessary to write or say "an" instead of "a."

_____

_____

_____

Using a Washing Machine

Teacher Notes

Lesson Focus

Punctuation

- Capital letters for sentence beginnings
- Periods
- Question marks
- Colons – recognition

Grammar

- Command verbs
- Words used as verbs or nouns

Spelling

- Confused words: to/too/two, of/off, your/yore
- Misspelled words

Vocabulary

- Compound words

Teacher Information

This procedure explains precisely how to use a washing machine.

Answers

Requirement**s**(:)
- water
- washing machine
- electricity supply
- items *to* be washed
- detergent

Metho**d**(:)
- **S**eparate light and dark colored items**.**
- **P**lace a load in machine without overloading**.**
- **A**dd correct amount *of* detergent**.**
- **C**lose machine**.**
- **S**et load size**.**
- **C**hoose correct water temperature**.**
- **S**elect washing program**.**
- **C**heck water is turned on**.**
- **I**nsert machine plug into socket**.**
- **T**urn on electricity supply**.**
- **S**tart machine**.**

Evaluatio**n**(:)
- **W**as *your* washing clean**?**

1. (a) Missing punctuation is in **bold type,** colons are circled.

2. (a) Spelling errors are in *italic type*. to, separate, of, your

3. (a) Command verbs are underlined. Separate, Place, Add, Close, Set, Choose, Select, Check, Insert, Turn on, Start

   (b) 11 command verbs

   (c) play, sleep, drink

   (d) Teacher check

4. (a) without, overload(ing)

Using a Washing Machine

Editing

❶ Punctuation

(a) The procedure needs 15 capital letters, 11 periods and 1 question mark. Circle 3 colons.

❷ Spelling

(a) Circle the correct word in each bracket.

❸ Grammar

A command verb tells us what to do.

(a) Underline all the command verbs in the text.

(b) How many are there? _____

Some words can be either verbs or nouns depending on their meaning within the sentence; for example:

<u>Walk</u> to the door. (verb)

We enjoyed our <u>walk</u>. (noun)

(c) Circle the words below that could be used as either a noun or a verb.

play   sleep   drink   open

(d) Choose one word and use it to write two sentences. Use it as a noun in one sentence and as a verb in the other.

- _____
  _____
- _____
  _____

❹ Vocabulary

Compound words are two words joined together as one.

(a) There are 2 compound words in the text. Find and circle each.

Read the procedure.

requirements:
- water
- washing machine
- electricity supply
- items (to/too/two) be washed
- detergent

method:
- (separate/seperate) light and dark colored items
- place a load in machine without overloading
- add correct amount (of/off) detergent
- close machine
- set load size
- choose correct water temperature
- select washing program
- check water is turned on
- insert machine plug into socket
- turn on electricity supply
- start machine

evaluation:
- was (your/yore) washing clean

My Siamese Cat

Teacher Notes

Lesson Focus

Punctuation

- Capital letters for sentence beginnings
- Capital letters for proper nouns
- Capital letters for the pronoun "I"
- Periods
- Commas in a list

Grammar

- Pronouns
- Adjectives

Spelling

- Confused words: one/won, by/buy, tail/tale
- Misspelled words

Writing

- Paragraphs

Teacher Information

Descriptions describe the characteristics, components or functions of specific living or non living things.

Answers

When **I** went to look at a *litter* of five kittens, ***they*** all looked so cute that **I** cuddled them all. **O**ne *kept* coming back to ***me***. **T**he owners said that ***he*** had obviously chosen ***me*** and that ***he*** *was* the *one* **I** should *buy*, so **I** did.

His full name is **K**wanlee **C**heong **H**oi, but ***we*** call ***him*** **C**heong. **H**e is *white* with chocolate-brown ears**,** face and *tail* and *bright* blue eyes**.** **L**ike all **S**iamese cats, ***he*** is sleek and elegant and ***he*** walks in a *proud* and aloof *manner*.

Cheong chose ***me*** and ***he*** makes it very clear that ***he*** is in charge. **H**e has trained ***me*** well, issuing ***his*** orders for food or attention in a very *loud* voice which is hard to ignore, especially *when* **I** am speaking on the *telephone*.

When **M**om picks up ***her*** keys, ***he*** races to the car and stretches out along the back window ledge *ready* to *enjoy* the drive**.**

Cheong is a wonderful pet and an important part of ***my*** life**.**

1. (a) Missing punctuation is in **bold type**.

2. (a) Spelling errors are in *italic type*. litter, kept, was, one, buy, white, tail, bright, proud, manner, loud, when, telephone, ready, enjoy

3. (a) Pronouns are in ***bold italic*** type.

   (b) he – his
   she – hers
   we – ours
   they – theirs
   it – its

   (c) Adjectives may include: white, chocolate-brown, proud, aloof, loud

   (d) Teacher check

4. (a) Paragraph 2.

My Siamese Cat

Editing

Read the description.

when i went to look at a (litter/litta) of five kittens, they all looked so cute that i cuddled them all one (keeped/kept) coming back to me the owners said that he had obviously chosen me and that he (wos/was) the (one/won) i should (by/buy), so i did

his full name is kwanlee cheong hoi, but we call him cheong he is (wite/white) with chocolate-brown ears face and (tale/tail) and (bright/brite) blue eyes like all siamese cats, he is sleek and elegant and he walks in a (prowd/proud) and aloof (manner/manna)

cheong chose me and he makes it very clear that he is in charge he has trained me well, issuing his orders for food or attention in a very (loud/lowd) voice which is hard to ignore, especially (wen/when) i am speaking on the (telephone/telaphone)

when mom picks up her keys, he races to the car and stretches out along the back window ledge (ready/reddy) to (injoy/enjoy) the drive

cheong is a wonderful pet and an important part of my life

❶ Punctuation
(a) The description needs 10 capital letters to start sentences, 9 periods, 6 capital letters for proper nouns, 5 for the word "I" and 1 comma in a list in paragraph 2.

❷ Spelling
(a) Circle the correct word in each bracket.

❸ Grammar
Pronouns are words used instead of nouns; for example, "I," "he," "they."

(a) Underline an example of a pronoun in each paragraph.

(b) Match the pronouns. One has been done for you.

he   hers
she   ours
we   his
they   its
it   theirs

Adjectives are used to describe nouns.

(c) List 4 of the adjectives used to describe the cat in the text.

_____ _____

_____ _____

(d) Write 6 other adjectives you would use to describe a cat.

_____ _____

_____ _____

_____ _____

❹ Writing
(a) Which paragraph describes Cheong's physical features? _____

Wonderwings

Teacher Notes

Lesson Focus

Punctuation
- Capital letters for sentence beginnings
- Periods
- Question marks
- Exclamation marks
- Commas in a list
- Grammatical commas

Spelling
- Confused words: soar/saw
- Misspelled words

Grammar
- Indefinite articles, "a" or "an"

Vocabulary
- Similes

Teacher Information

An exposition is written to persuade others to think or do something. Expositions use persuasive language.

Answers

> **I**magine soaring high in the sky, experiencing the thrill of *flight* …
>
> **H**ave you ever wished you had the *ability* to fly like a bird**?** To just flap your arms and take off into the open sky? **W**ell, with WONDERWINGS, now you can!
>
> **A**erodynamically designed**,** nonpolluting, fully tested WONDERWINGS can help you take to the skies. **S**imply strap them onto your back, and you're up**,** up and away! **S**o simple, anyone can try it**.** **I**t's easy**!**
>
> 100% *feather*-lined WONDERWINGS sold out in other *countries* within days of being advertised—don't miss out**!**
>
> **W**ith WONDERWINGS**,** you can *soar* like an *eagle***.** **O**rder your pair today!

1. Missing punctuation is in **bold type**.
2. (a) Spelling errors are in *italic type*.
   flight, ability, feather, countries, soar, eagle
3. (a) a bird, an eagle
   (b) (i) a penguin (ii) an owl
       (iii) an ant   (iv) a kitten
4. (a) Teacher check

Wonderwings

Read the exposition in the form of an advertisement.

Editing

imagine soaring high in the sky, experiencing the thrill of flite ...

have you ever wished you had the abilitee to fly like a bird To just flap your arms and take off into the open sky? well, with WONDERWINGS, now you can!

aerodynamically designed nonpolluting, fully tested WONDERWINGS can help you take to the skies simply strap them onto your back, and you're up up and away! so simple, anyone can try it it's easy

100% fether-lined WONDERWINGS sold out in other contries within days of being advertised— don't miss out

with WONDERWINGS you can saw like an egle order your pair today!

❶ Punctuation
(a) The exposition needs 9 capital letters used for beginning sentences, 3 periods, 2 exclamation marks and 1 question mark.

(b) Two commas are missing in paragraph 3 and one comma in paragraph 5.

❷ Spelling
(a) Six words are misspelled. Write the correct spelling.

_____   _____

_____   _____

_____   _____

❸ Grammar
(a) Write the words in the text that follow "a" and "an."

a _____

an _____

(b) Write "a" or "an" in front of these words.

(i) ____ penguin   (ii) ____ owl

(iii) ____ ant   (iv) ____ kitten

❹ Vocabulary
Similes compare one thing to another; for example, "like a bird," "like an eagle" and "as cold as ice."

(a) Write a simile to complete these sentences.

(i) The baby's skin is as

_____

(ii) My dog acts like

_____

(iii) The wind felt as

_____

(iv) The lake looks like

_____

Swimming Gold!

Teacher Notes

Lesson Focus

Punctuation

- Capital letters for sentence beginnings
- Capital letters for the pronoun "I"
- Capital letters for proper nouns
- Periods
- Grammatical commas
- Colons – recognition

Spelling

- Silent letters

Grammar

- Verbs – tenses
- Pronouns

Teacher Information

A recount is a retelling of events in time order.

Answers

> **S**aturday, **M**arch 15**:** **T**oday has been the best day of the year so far for me**.** **T**he club swimming championships were held and for the first time **I** was a competitor**.** **I** was both <u>excited</u> and <u>scared</u>**,** all at the same time**.**
>
> **M**y event was the 200-meter individual medley**.** **A**s **I** <u>climbed</u> on to the block and <u>waited</u> for the starter's gun**,** **I** <u>imagined</u> **I** was in an **O**lympic final**.** **I** knew **I** wasn't the fastest over 50 meters in any of the individual strokes**,** but with the four of them together**,** **I** had a good chance of winning**.** **M**y dive felt perfect and **I** was under way**.** **E**ach stroke felt smooth and strong**,** but **I** believe it was the hours **I** spent practicing my turns that really made the difference**.** **I**n less than four minutes**,** the gold was mine**.**

1. (a) Missing punctuation and punctuation to identify is in **bold type**.
   (b) (i) 9 capitals for sentence beginnings (ii) 12 for the pronoun "I"
      (iii) 3 for proper nouns
   (c) The 6 commas are circled.
   (d) The colon is circled.

2. (a)

Silent "b"	Silent "k"	Silent "g"	Silent "n"
climb	know	gnome	autumn
thumb	knight	gnat	column
lamb	kneel	gnarled	hymn

3. (a) The past tense verbs with "ed" are <u>underlined</u>.
      excited, scared, climbed, waited, imagined
   (b) (i) to hold – held   (ii) to know – knew   (iii) to have – had
      (iv) to feel – felt   (v) to spend – spent
   (c) me, my, mine

Swimming Gold!

Editing

Read the recount.

saturday, march 15: today has been the best day of the year so far for me the club swimming championships were held and for the first time i was a competitor i was both excited and scared, all at the same time

my event was the 200-meter individual medley as i climbed on to the block and waited for the starter's gun, i imagined i was in an olympic final i knew i wasn't the fastest over 50 meters in any of the individual strokes, but with the four of them together, i had a good chance of winning my dive felt perfect and i was under way each stroke felt smooth and strong, but i believe it was the hours i spent practicing my turns that really made the difference in less than four minutes, the gold was mine

❶ Punctuation

(a) The recount needs 21 capital letters and 9 periods.

(b) How many capital letters are used for:

(i) sentence beginnings? _____

(ii) the pronoun "I"? _____

(iii) proper nouns? _____

(c) Circle all the commas. How many are there? _____

(d) Circle the colon.

❷ Spelling

*Some words have silent letters; e.g., **k**new.*

(a) Write in the missing letter.

Silent "b"	Silent "k"	Silent "g"	Silent "n"
clim__	__now	__nome	autum__
thum__	__night	__nat	colum__
lam__	__neel	__narled	hym__

❸ Grammar

The past tense of verbs is often formed by adding "ed" to the word.

(a) Underline the 5 verbs with the past tense formed this way.

(b) In the text, find the past tense of these verbs.

(i) to hold _____

(ii) to know _____

(iii) to have _____

(iv) to feel _____

(v) to spend _____

Pronouns are used in place of nouns. In this text, the pronoun "I" is used many times as the writer is talking about herself.

(c) What are the other 3 pronouns she uses when talking about herself?

_____ _____

_____

Dinosaur Feast

Teacher Notes

Lesson Focus

Punctuation

- Capital letters at the beginning of each line of a poem
- Periods

Grammar

- Pronouns
- Conjunctions
- Collective nouns

Spelling

- Confused words: threw/through, herd/heard, prey/pray, two/to/too
- Misspelled words

Vocabulary

- Antonyms

Teacher Information

Narratives tell a story in a sequence of events.

Answers

The dinosaur moved *through* the forest**.**	through
He *sniffed* the air to the west**.**	sniffed
He spotted his goal —a *herd* of beasts	herd
Enjoying their own grassy *feast***.**	feast
He lowered *his* head and started to run	his
On gigantic, *bony* feet**.**	bony
His *gaping* jaws took aim and soon	gaping
The *prey* was his to eat**.**	prey
A bite or *two* and then the hunter	two
Began his own *meaty* feast**.**	meaty

1. (a) Missing punctuation is in **bold type**.
2. (a) Spelling errors are in *italic type*.
   through, sniffed, herd, feast, his, bony, gaping, prey, two, meaty
3. (a) he, his, their
   (b) and
   (c) He lowered his head. He started to run.
   (d) a herd
4. (a) (i) west (ii) gigantic
   (iii) started/began

Dinosaur Feast

Editing

Read the narrative poem.

the dinosaur moved threw the forest _____

he snifed the air to the west _____

he spotted his goal—a heard of beasts _____

enjoying their own grassy feest _____

he lowered hiz head and started to run _____

on gigantic, boney feet _____

his gapping jaws took aim and soon _____

the pray was his to eat _____

a bite or too and then the hunter _____

began his own meety feast _____

❶ Punctuation

(a) The narrative poem needs 10 capital letters and 6 periods.

❷ Spelling

(a) Write the misspelled words correctly at the end of each line.

❸ Grammar

Pronouns are words used instead of nouns; for example, "she," "it," "they," "you."

(a) Circle 3 different pronouns which can be found in the poem.

Conjunctions are words which join words, groups of words and sentences. They include words such as: and, because, so, if, when, that, as soon as.

(b) Write the joining word used in the poem.

_____

(c) Write the two small sentences which make up this sentence.

"He lowered his head and he started to run."

_____

_____

Collective nouns are the names given to particular groups.

(d) What collective noun is given to the group of beasts in the poem?

_____

❹ Vocabulary

(a) Find opposites in the text for these words.

(i) east _____

(ii) tiny _____

(iii) finished _____

Volcanoes

Teacher Notes

Lesson Focus

Punctuation

- Capital letters for sentence beginnings
- Capital letters for proper nouns
- Periods
- Commas in a list
- Apostrophe for possession
- Colons – recognition

Spelling

- Confused words: through/threw, some/sum, which/witch, new/knew
- Misspelled words
- Plurals – adding "s" and "es"

Grammar

- Verb tenses – present and future

Teacher Information

An explanation analyzes how something works, is made, or how or why things happen.

Answers

Volcanoes are places on the **E**arth**'**s surface *through which* molten rock, called magma, and gas from far below the surface erupt**.**

Volcanic eruptions can be violent, spilling hot lava**,** ash**,** dust**,** gas and cinders over large areas**.**

They can trigger tsunamis**,** earthquakes**,** floods**,** rockfalls and mudflows**.** **E**ruptions have caused *some* of the worst disasters in *history*, *killing* thousands of people**.**

Categories of volcanoes include**:** active, dormant (sleeping) and extinct (no longer active)**.**

Every time a volcano erupts it becomes bigger, because as the lava cools it forms a *new* layer of rock**.**

Although our understanding of volcanoes has increased, predicting *when* they will erupt and limiting the damage they *cause* is still difficult**.**

1. (a) Missing punctuation and punctuation to identify is in **bold type**.
   (b) The colon is circled.
2. (a) Spelling errors are in *italic type*. through, which, some, history, killing, new, when, cause
   (b) (i) volcanoes (or volcanos)
       (ii) disasters
       (iii) eruptions
3. (a) (i) erupted
       (ii) included
       (iii) caused
       (iv) triggered
       (v) were
       (vi) became
   (b) (i) will cause
       (ii) will cool
       (iii) will form
       (iv) will be

Volcanoes

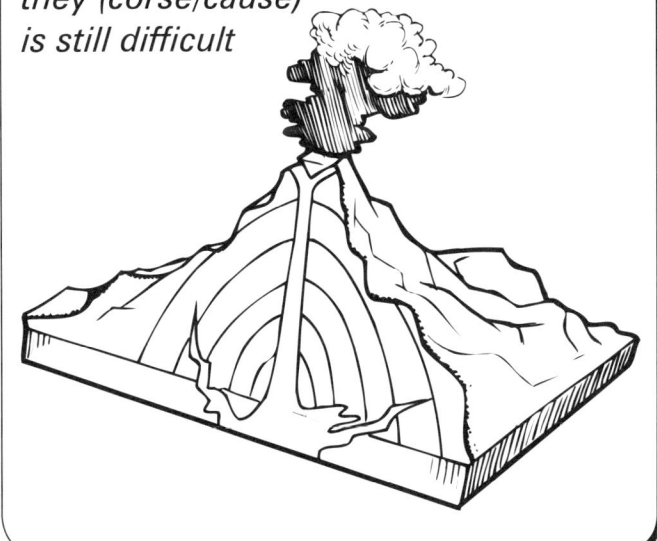

Editing

Read the explanation.

volcanoes are places on the earths surface (through/threw) (witch/which) molten rock, called magma, and gas from far below the surface erupt

volcanic eruptions can be violent, spilling hot lava ash dust gas and cinders over large areas

they can trigger tsunamis earthquakes floods rockfalls and mudflows eruptions have caused (some/sum) of the worst disasters in (historie/history), (killing/kiling) thousands of people

categories of volcanoes include: active dormant (sleeping) and extinct (no longer active)

every time a volcano erupts it becomes bigger, because as the lava cools it forms a (knew/new) layer of rock

although our understanding of volcanoes has increased, predicting (when/wen) they will erupt and limiting the damage they (corse/cause) is still difficult

❶ Punctuation
(a) The explanation needs 8 capital letters, 7 periods, 7 commas to separate items in a list and 1 apostrophe for possession.

(b) Circle the colon.

❷ Spelling
(a) Cross out the incorrectly spelled words.

When singular words are made plural, we can add "s" or "es"; e.g., "plants," "potatoes."

(b) Write the plural for these words.

(i) volcano _____

(ii) disaster _____

(iii) eruption _____

❸ Grammar
(a) Change these present tense verbs used in the explanation to the past tense.

Present tense	Past tense
(i) erupt	
(ii) include	
(iii) cause	
(iv) trigger	
(v) are	
(vi) becomes	

(b) Write these verbs in the future tense.

(i) cause _____

(ii) cools _____

(iii) forms _____

(iv) are _____

The Trojan Horse

Teacher Notes

Lesson Focus

Punctuation
- Capital letters for proper nouns
- Periods
- Grammatical commas

Grammar
- Verb tenses – past tense
- Adjectives
- Nouns – common nouns, plural nouns

Spelling
- Confused words: quiet/quite, sale/sail, bought/brought
- Misspelled words

Vocabulary
- Synonyms

Teacher Information

A recount is a retelling of past events in time order.

Answers

Queen **H**elen of **G**reece was kidnapped by **P**rince **P**aris who took her back to his home in **T**roy**.** The **G**reek people were very *upset* and <u>sent</u> **U**lysses and his warriors to **T**roy to get their queen back**.**

Athena, the goddess of war, <u>told</u> **U**lysses to build a huge wooden horse and to leave it outside the gates of **T**roy**.** The **G**reeks *pretended* to leave **T**roy, but *instead* they hid inside the huge horse**.**

The **T**rojans <u>discovered</u> the horse and <u>*brought*</u> it into their city**.** Believing the war was over**,** they had a huge celebration**.** *Afterwards***,** when everyone was tired**,** they all fell asleep**.**

When all was *quiet*, the **G**reeks <u>opened</u> the wooden horse and attacked the **T**rojans**.** They <u>rescued</u> **Q**ueen **H**elen and set *sail* for their home in **G**reece**.**

1. Missing punctuation is in **bold type**.
2. (a) Spelling errors are in *italic type*.
   upset, pretended, instead, brought, afterwards, quiet, sail
3. (a) The past tense of each verb is <u>underlined</u>.
   to send – sent, to tell – told, to bring – brought,
   to discover – discovered, to open – opened, to rescue – rescued
   (b) The first 3 are irregular, complete word change. The last 3 are regular, add -ed.
   (c) (i) huge, wooden
   (ii) home, people, warriors, queen
   (iii) Possible answers: warriors, gates
4. (a) Teacher check; possible answers include: enormous, gigantic, immense

The Trojan Horse

Editing

Read the recount.

Queen helen of greece was kidnapped by prince paris who took her back to his home in troy The greek people were very (upset/ubset) and sent ulysses and his warriors to troy to get their queen back

Athena, the goddess of war, told ulysses to build a huge wooden horse and to leave it outside the gates of troy The greeks (pretended/pertended) to leave troy, but (instead/insted) they hid inside the huge horse

The trojans discovered the horse and (bought/brought) it into their city Believing the war was over they had a huge celebration (Afterwoods/Afterwards) when everyone was tired they all fell asleep

When all was (quiet/quite), the greeks opened the wooden horse and attacked the trojans They rescued queen helen and set (sale/sail) for their home in greece

❶ Punctuation

(a) The recount needs 18 capital letters for proper nouns and 9 periods.

(b) Three commas are missing from paragraph 3.

❷ Spelling

(a) Circle the correct word in each bracket.

❸ Grammar

A recount is usually written in the past tense, as the events have already occurred.

(a) In the text, underline the past tense of these verbs and write them below.

(to send)   (to tell)   (to bring)

_____   _____   _____

(to discover)   (to open)   (to rescue)

_____   _____   _____

(b) What is the difference between the past tense of the top three verbs and the last three verbs you wrote?

_____

_____

(c) From the text, list:

(i) 2 adjectives from paragraph 2.

_____   _____

(ii) 4 common nouns from paragraph 1.

_____   _____

_____   _____

(iii) 1 plural noun _____

❹ Vocabulary

(a) Write 2 synonyms (words with the same meaning) for "huge."

_____   _____

Pottery Places

Teacher Notes

Lesson Focus

Punctuation
- Capital letters for sentence beginnings
- Periods
- Commas in a list
- Colons – recognition

Grammar
- Adverbs
- Pronouns

Spelling
- Misspelled words
- Silent letters

Writing
- Rewriting a list as a sentence

Teacher Information

A procedure shows how something is done. Instructions are written using command verbs, usually at the beginning of sentences.

Answers

Materials**:**
- *pencil*
- paper
- string
- *skewer*
- knife
- *scissors*
- rolling pin
- a ball of clay
- carving tools
- 2 flat**,** thin *pieces* of wood

Instructions**:**

1. **R**oll the clay between the *pieces* of wood until it is an even *thickness*.
2. **U**se paper about the same size as the clay to draw a house shape**.**
3. **C**ut out the house**,** place it on the clay and *trace* around it with the *knife*. **R**emove the extra clay**.**
4. **U**se the tools or excess clay to add detail to the house shape**.**
5. **P**oke a hole near the top with the skewer**.**
6. **A**llow to dry and hang by the string to display**.**

1. (a) Missing punctuation and punctuation to identify is in **bold type**.
   (b) The colons are circled.
2. (a) Spelling errors are in *italic type*.
   pencil, scissors, skewer, pieces, thickness, trace, knife
   (b) knife
   (c) Teacher check
3. (a) Teacher check
   (b) (i) girl: she, her, hers
       (ii) boy: he, him, his
       (iii) parents: they, them, theirs
       (iv) toy: it, its
4. Teacher check

Pottery Places

Read the procedure.

materials:
- pensil
- sissors
- paper
- knife
- rolling pin
- scewer
- string
- a ball of clay
- carving tools
- 2 flat thin pieces of wood

instructions:
1. roll the clay between the peices of wood until it is an even thikness

2. use paper about the same size as the clay to draw a house shape
3. cut out the house place it on the clay and trase around it with the nife remove the extra clay
4. use the tools or excess clay to add detail to the house shape
5. poke a hole near the top with the skewer
6. allow to dry and hang by the string to display

❶ Punctuation

(a) The procedure needs 9 capital letters, 7 periods and 2 commas between words in lists.

(b) Circle the colons.

❷ Spelling

(a) Seven different words are misspelled. Underline each, then write the correct spelling.

_____

_____

_____

Editing

(b) Which word needed a silent "k"?

_____

(c) Write two more silent "k" words.

_____ _____

❸ Grammar

Adverbs add meaning to verbs.

(a) Write adverbs to match these verbs.

(i) roll _____

(ii) place _____

(iii) cut _____

Pronouns may be used in place of a noun. In the text, "it" is used to mean "the clay" or "the house."

(b) Write a pronoun to match each of these words:

(i) girl _____ (ii) boy _____

(iii) parents _____ (iv) toy _____

❹ Writing

(a) Complete this sentence using commas to list the materials needed to make coffee.

I will need _____

_____

_____

_____ .

Monkeynaut

Teacher Notes

Lesson Focus

Punctuation
- Capital letters for sentence beginnings
- Capital letters for proper nouns
- Periods
- Grammatical commas

Grammar
- Verb tenses

Spelling
- Misspelled words

Vocabulary
- Compound words
- Synonyms
- Shortened forms

Teacher Information

A recount is a retelling of past events in time order.

Answers

> **G**ordo**,** a squirrel monkey**,** was *launched* into space by the **U**nited **S**tates Army on **D**ecember 13, 1958, inside the nosecone of a spacecraft called Jupiter AM-13. ***S**cientists* wanted to see if a human being could survive a flight into space**.**
>
> **G**ordo wore a *special* helmet and was strapped into a chair**.** **H**e had buttons and levers to press during the flight to see if he could perform jobs as well as survive the *flight***.**
>
> **G**ordo survived the flight but**,** when the spacecraft touched down in the **A**tlantic **O**cean**,** he *drowned* because the device that was supposed to keep him *afloat* did not work**.**

1. (a) Missing punctuation is in **bold type**.
2. (a) Spelling errors are in *italic type*.
    launched, Scientists, special, flight, drowned, afloat
3. (a) Answers may include:
    (i) is launching, launches
    (ii) is strapped, straps, is strapping
    (iii) survives, survive, is surviving, are surviving
    (iv) is supposed to
4. (a) nosecone, spacecraft
   (b) Teacher check
   (c) (i) December   (ii) United States
   (d) (i) Rd.   (ii) Ave.

Monkeynaut

Editing

Read the recount.

gordo a squirrel monkey was lornched into space by the united states Army on december 13, 1958, inside the nosecone of a spacecraft called Jupiter AM-13 sientists wanted to see if a human being could survive a flight into space

gordo wore a speshl helmet and was strapped into a chair he had buttons and levers to press during the flight to see if he could perform jobs as well as survive the flite

gordo survived the flight but when the spacecraft touched down in the atlantic ocean he drownd because the device that was supposed to keep him ufloat did not work and sank

❶ Punctuation
(a) The recount needs 10 capital letters (8 for proper nouns), 5 periods and 4 missing commas (2 in the first sentence and 2 in the last).

❷ Spelling
(a) Six words are misspelled. Underline them, then write the correct spelling.

_____   _____

_____   _____

_____   _____

❸ Grammar
Recounts use verbs in the past tense.

(a) Change the verbs from past tense to present tense.

   (i) was launched _____

   (ii) was strapped _____

   (iii) survived _____

   (iv) was supposed to _____

❹ Vocabulary
(a) Write 2 compound words from the text.

_____

Synonyms are words which have nearly the same meaning as another word.

(b) Write synonyms for the words below.

   (i) launched _____

   (ii) called _____

   (iii) survive _____

   (iv) perform _____

   (v) touched down _____

Shortened forms of words and groups of words can be used.

(c) What words in the text do these shortened forms represent?

   (i) Dec. _____

   (ii) US _____

(d) Shorten these words.

   (i) Road _____ (ii) Avenue _____

The Bear and the Tourists

Teacher Notes

Lesson Focus

Punctuation

- Capital letters for sentence beginnings
- Periods
- Question marks
- Exclamation marks
- Direct speech

Spelling

- Confused words: through/threw, road/rode, would/wood, its/it's, for/four, bear/bare
- Misspelled words

Grammar

- Adjectives
- Adverbs

Teacher Information

A narrative tells about a series of events and often involves fictitious characters.

Answers

Two tourists were traveling along a winding road *through* a thick *forest*. **A**s they turned a bend in the *road*, they came face to face with a very large brown bear.

One of the men quickly climbed a tree and cleverly concealed himself in *its* thick branches. **T**he other, fearing he *would* be attacked, threw himself flat on the ground. **W**hen the bear approached and *sniffed* him all over, the man held his breath and *didn't* move, feigning the appearance of death.

The bear soon left him, *for* as it is said, a bear will not touch a dead *body*.

When the bear was gone, the other tourist slid down the tree and jokingly *asked* his companion, "What did the *bear* secretly whisper in your ear?"

His *friend* replied, "He gave me this piece of *advice*—never travel with a friend who selfishly deserts you at the first sign of danger!"

1. (a) Missing punctuation is in **bold type**.
   (b) Direct speech is underlined.
2. (a) Spelling errors are in *italic type*.
      through, forest, road, its, would, sniffed, didn't, for, body, asked, bear, friend, advice
   (b) (i) I think **it's** a good fable.
       (ii) The bear only sniffed **its** prey.
3. (a) (i) bear   (ii) road
       (iii) body   (iv) forest
       (v) bear   (vi) sign
   (b) (i) quickly   (ii) soon
       (iii) cleverly (iv) jokingly

The Bear and the Tourists

Editing

Read the narrative.

two tourists were traveling along a winding road (threw/through) a thick (forest/forrest) as they turned a bend in the (rode/road), they came face to face with a very large brown bear

one of the men quickly climbed a tree and cleverly concealed himself in (its/it's) thick branches the other, fearing he (wood/would) be attacked, threw himself flat on the ground when the bear approached and (sniffed/snifed) him all over, the man held his breath and (did'nt/didn't) move, feigning the appearance of death

the bear soon left him, (four/for) as it is said, a bear will not touch a dead (body/bode)

when the bear was gone, the other tourist slid down the tree and jokingly (asked/askt) his companion, "What did the (bare/bear) secretly whisper in your ear"

his (freind/friend) replied, "He gave me this piece of (advise/advice)—never travel with a friend who selfishly deserts you at the first sign of danger"

❶ Punctuation

(a) The narrative needs 8 capital letters, 6 periods, 1 question mark and 1 exclamation mark.

(b) Underline the words spoken by the two tourists, using a different color for each.

❷ Spelling

(a) Circle the correct word in each bracket.

*Its or it's? Remember that "it's" is a contraction and can **only** be used in place of the words "it is" or "it has."*

(b) Circle the correct spelling in each sentence.

   (i) I think (it's/its) a good fable.

   (ii) The bear only sniffed (it's/its) prey.

❸ Grammar

Adjectives can describe nouns.

(a) Find the nouns in the fable to match these adjectives.

   (i) large _____   (ii) winding _____

   (iii) dead _____   (iv) thick _____

   (v) brown _____   (vi) first _____

Adverbs can tell how, when or where something happens. They can describe verbs.

(b) Find the adverbs in the fable to match these verbs.

   (i) climbed _____

   (ii) left _____

   (iii) concealed _____

   (iv) asked _____

How Plants Drink

Teacher Notes

Lesson Focus

Punctuation

- Capital letters for sentence beginnings
- Periods
- Question marks
- Grammatical commas

Spelling

- Confused words: no/know
- Misspelled words
- Suffixes – Rule: "e" goes away when "ing" comes to stay.

Grammar

- Conjunctions

Teacher Information

An explanation analyzes how something works, is made, or how or why things happen.

Answers

When we cut flowers and place them in a vase of water, how do we *know* that the plants *drink* the water**?**

You could *measure* the amount of water left in the vase, or you may *like* to try *placing* a short-stemmed white carnation in a *glass* of water with food coloring added and observing what happens**.**

After a few hours, the flower will change *color* because plants have vascular tissue (veins) which transport water and *sugars* around the plant**.** **I**f you look carefully at the flower, you will see the tiny veins which carry water to each part of the flower petal**.**

If you split the stem of one flower and stand each half in *different* colored water, each part will take the color of the water it is in, showing that the tiny tubes *lead* to specific parts of the flower**.**

1. (a) Missing punctuation and punctuation to identify is in **bold type**.
   (b) The 5 commas are circled.
2. (a) Spelling errors are in *italic type*.
   when, know, drink, measure, like, placing, glass, color, sugars, different, lead
   (b) (i) placing   (ii) measuring
       (iii) liking   (iv) tubing
       (v) observing   (vi) changing
3. (a) Answers may include:
   (i) If you buy the tickets today, you can go to the movies.
   (ii) I didn't water the garden because I thought it would rain.
   (iii) You can watch TV or you can read a book.

How Plants Drink

Editing

Read the explanation.

(when/wen) we cut flowers and place them in a vase of water, how do we (no/know) that the plants (drink/drinck) the water

you could (mesure/measure) the amount of water left in the vase, **or** *you may (like/lick) to try (placing/placeing) a short-stemmed white carnation in a (glas/glass) of water with food coloring added* **and** *observing what happens*

after a few hours, the flower will change (color/colour) **because** *plants have vascular tissue (veins) which transport water and (sugars/sugers) around the plant* **if** *you look carefully at the flower, you will see the tiny veins which carry water to each part of the flower petal*

if you split the stem of one flower **and** *stand each half in (diferent/different) colored water, each part will take the color of the water it is in, showing that the tiny tubes (leed/lead) to specific parts of the flower*

❶ Punctuation

(a) The explanation needs 5 capital letters, 4 periods and 1 question mark.

(b) Circle the 5 commas.

❷ Spelling

(a) Circle the correct word in each bracket.

Before adding the suffix "-ing" to words ending with a silent "e," the "e" is dropped.

(b) Add "-ing" to these words:

(i) place _____

(ii) measure _____

(iii) like _____

(iv) tube _____

(v) observe _____

(vi) change _____

❸ Grammar

The words in bold type in the explanation are conjunctions (joining words).

(a) Choose a conjunction to join each pair of sentences.

(i) You can go to the movies. Buy the tickets today.

_____

_____

(ii) I didn't water the garden. I thought it would rain.

_____

_____

(iii) You can watch TV. You can read a book.

_____

_____

My Pop

Teacher Notes

Lesson Focus

Punctuation

- Capital letters at the beginning of each line of a poem
- Periods
- Exclamation marks
- Apostrophes in contractions
- Apostrophes for possession

Grammar

- Pronouns
- Apostrophes in contractions
- Apostrophes for possession
- Adjectives

Spelling

- Confused words: hare/hair, were/wear, to/too/two, no/know
- Misspelled words
- Silent letters

Vocabulary

- Enrichment – word meanings

Teacher Information

Many different types of poems include descriptions. These include shape, pattern, syllable, sense and string poems as well as haiku and cinquain.

Answers

> **I** love my pop**.**
> **H**e**'**s really tops**!**
> **H**is *hair* is gray**.**
> **I**t**'**ll stay that way**!**
> **H**is face is wrinkled,
> **B**ut his eyes still twinkle**!**
> **H**is body is lumpy**.**
> **H**is *knees* are bumpy**.**
>
> **H**e loves to *wear* old, baggy shorts**.**
> **A**ll our protests come to nought**!**
> **H**e may look strange *to* others**'** eyes
> **A**nd act a bit odd—but I tell no lies**!**
> **H**e**'**s the best grown-up that I *know***.**
> **A**ll care and no responsibility—that**'**s my pop**'**s motto**!**

1. (a) Missing punctuation is **bold type**.
2. (a) Spelling errors are in *italic type*.
   hair, knees, wear, to, know
   (b) knees/know
   (c) (i) limb, b   (ii) knot, k
       (iii) ghost, h   (iv) island, s
3. (a) An example of each of these pronouns should be circled: I, my, He, His, It, our
   (b) (i) boys' or boy's shirts
       (ii) children's toys
       (iii) mothers' or mother's babies

(c) (i) wrinkled   (ii) bumpy
    (iii) gray   (iv) lumpy

4. (a) Teacher check, possible explanations may include:
   (i) expression of disapproval
   (ii) nothing, zero
   (iii) a duty or care
   (iv) different
   (v) guiding principle

My Pop

Read the poem.

i love my pop
hes really tops
his (hare/hair) is gray
itll stay that way
his face is wrinkled,
but his eyes still twinkle
his body is lumpy
his (knees/nees) are bumpy

he loves to (were/wear) old, baggy shorts
all our protests come to nought
he may look strange (to/too/two) others eyes
and act a bit odd—but I tell no lies
hes the best grown-up that I (no/know)
all care and no responsibility—thats my
pops motto

Editing

❶ Punctuation

(a) The poem needs 14 capital letters, 6 periods, 5 exclamation marks and 6 apostrophes (4 in contractions and 2 to show possession).

❷ Spelling

(a) Circle the correct word in each bracket.

(b) Which word was missing a silent letter? _____

(c) Circle the silent letters in these words.

   (i) limb   (ii) knot

   (iii) ghost   (iv) island

❸ Grammar

Pronouns are used in place of nouns; e.g., "I," "his."

(a) There are 6 different pronouns used in the poem. Circle an example of each.

To show possession, the apostrophe goes after the owner or owners; for example, men's shirts, ladies' shoes.

(b) Add the apostrophe in the correct place in the groups of words below.

   (i) boys shirts   (ii) childrens toys

   (iii) mothers babies

(c) Write the adjective that describes each of these features of "My Pop."

   (i) face _____

   (ii) knees _____

   (iii) hair _____

   (iv) body _____

❹ Vocabulary

(a) Explain the meaning of the following words.

   (i) protests _____

   (ii) nought _____

   (iii) responsibility _____

   (iv) odd _____

   (v) motto _____

Biography of Sir Edmund Hillary
Teacher Notes

Lesson Focus

Punctuation
- Capital letters for sentence beginnings
- Capital letters for proper nouns
- Capital letters for titles
- Periods
- Grammatical commas
- Commas in a list

Spelling
- Misspelled words
- Silent letters

Grammar
- Pronouns
- Conjunctions

Teacher Information

A biography is a recount of a person's life and achievements.

Answers

> **S**ir **E**dmund **H**illary was born in 1919 in **N**ew **Z**ealand**,** where he became very *interested* in mountain climbing**.** **H**e climbed *mountains* in **N**ew **Z**ealand**,** the **A**lps and the **H**imalayas**.**
>
> **H**e joined two expeditions to climb **M**ount **E**verest in 1951 and 1952**.** **I**n 1953 he joined another *expedition* to **E**verest**.** **O**nly two of the climbers were able to continue**.** **T**he others had to go back because they had become exhausted in the high *altitude***.** **H**illary and **T**enzing **N**orgay**,** a climber from **N**epal**,** reached the top of the mountain on **M**ay 29, 1953**.**
>
> **W**hen **H**illary returned to **B**ritain with the other climbers**,** he was knighted by **Q**ueen **E**lizabeth II**.**

1. (a) Missing punctuation is in **bold type**.
   (b) (i) Mrs.   (ii) Dr.   (iii) Mr.   (iv) Reverend/Father/Rabbi/Imam, etc.
   (v) Sergeant/Captain/Lieutenant/Major/General/Private, etc.
2. (a) Possible answers: climbed, climb, climbers, exhausted, climbing, knighted
   (b) Spelling errors are in *italic type*.
   Zealand, interested, mountains, expedition, altitude
3. Answers may include: (a) he, they
   (b) where, because, and, when
   (c) Teacher check, possible answers:
   - Hillary became famous because/after/when he climbed Mt Everest.
   - After/Because/When he climbed Mt Everest, Hillary became famous.

Biography of Sir Edmund Hillary

Editing

Read the recount.

sir edmund hillary was born in 1919 in new zeeland, where he became very intrested in mountain climbing he climbed mountins in new zealand the alps and the himalayas

he joined two expeditions to climb mount everest in 1951 and 1952 in 1953 he joined another expedishon to everest only two of the climbers were able to continue the others had to go back because they had become exhausted in the high altitood hillary and tenzing norgay a climber from nepal reached the top of the mountain on may 29, 1953

when hillary returned to britain with the other climbers he was knighted by queen elizabeth II

❶ Punctuation

(a) The biography needs 27 capital letters (21 for proper nouns), 8 periods and 5 commas.

"Sir" is a person's title. It has a capital letter.

(b) Write titles for these people:

(i) a married woman

_____

(ii) a person trained to practice medicine

_____

(iii) a man

_____

(iv) a religious leader

_____

(v) a person in the army (rank)

_____

❷ Spelling

(a) Write 4 words in the text which have silent letters.

_____
_____
_____

(b) Underline the 5 misspelled words and write the correct spellings below.

_____
_____
_____

❸ Grammar

Pronouns may be used in place of a noun.

(a) Circle two pronouns in the recount.

Conjunctions join two smaller sentences.

(b) Underline 2 conjunctions in the text.

(c) Use a conjunction to join these.

Hillary became famous. He climbed Mt. Everest.

_____
_____

Kakadu National Park

Teacher Notes

Lesson Focus

Punctuation

- Capital letters for sentence beginnings
- Capital letters for proper nouns
- Periods

Spelling

- Confused words: sea/see, great/grate
- Misspelled words

Grammar

- Compound verbs
- Verbs – present and past tense

Vocabulary

- Compound words

Teacher Information

Reports give facts clearly without unnecessary information or opinions.

Answers

> **K**akadu is the *largest* land-based park in **A**ustralia**.**   largest
> **L**ocated in the far north of the **N**orthern **T**erritory,   Northern
> **K**akadu was *once* part of a shallow sea, but it is   once
> now a *vibrant* land with fascinating wildlife**.**   vibrant
>
> **A**boriginal **A**ustralians have lived in the   Australians
> **K**akadu area for more than 40,000 years**.** *Some*   Some
> of the best *collections* of rock paintings   collections
> can be found in this *area***.**   area
>
> ***T**housands* of tourists are attracted to **K**akadu   Thousands
> each year, many to *see* the wonderland   see
> of wildlife such as the *saltwater* crocodiles**.**   saltwater
>
> **O**ne of **A**ustralia's most *famous* parks, **K**akadu   famous
> is renowned for its *great* natural beauty**.**   great

1. (a) Missing punctuation is in **bold type**.
   (b) 11
2. (a) Spelling errors are in *italic type*.
   largest, Northern, once, vibrant, Australians, Some, collections, area, Thousands, see, saltwater, famous, great
   (b) (i) **It's** raining.   (ii) I think **it's** sad.   (iii) What is **its** name?
3. (a) Possible answers include: is, located, can be found, are attracted, is renowned
   (b) was
   (c) Possible answers: can be found, are attracted, is renowned
4. (a) land-based, wildlife, wonderland, saltwater

Kakadu National Park

Editing

Read the report.

kakadu <u>is</u> the largist land-based park in australia _____

<u>located</u> in the far north of the northen territory, _____

kakadu <u>was</u> wuns part of a shallow sea, but it <u>is</u> _____

now a vibrent land with fascinating wildlife _____

aboriginal australiens have lived in the _____

kakadu area for more than 40,000 years sum _____

of the best collecshons of rock paintings _____

<u>can be found</u> in this erea _____

thousands of tourists <u>are attracted</u> to kakadu _____

each year, many to sea the wonderland _____

of wildlife such as the saltwata crocodiles _____

one of australia's most famos parks, kakadu _____

<u>is renowned</u> for its grate natural beauty _____

❶ Punctuation
(a) The report needs 15 capital letters and 6 periods.

(b) How many capital letters were needed for proper nouns? _____

❷ Spelling
(a) Underline the spelling mistake in each line of the text and write the correction at the end of the line.

"It's" is a contraction and can only be used in place of the words, "it is" and "it has."

(b) Choose the correct spelling.

(i) _____ raining.

(ii) I think _____ sad.

(iii) What is _____ name?

❸ Grammar
There are 7 verbs (doing words) underlined.

(a) Find 2 present tense verbs.

_____ and _____

(b) Find 1 past tense verb. _____

(c) Write 2 compound verbs (verbs with more than one word) underlined in the report.

_____ _____

❹ Vocabulary
(a) Write 4 compound words, hyphenated and unhyphenated, used in this report.

_____ _____

_____ _____

Water and the Body

Teacher Notes

Lesson Focus

Punctuation
- Capital letters for sentence beginnings
- Periods
- Commas in a list
- Exclamation marks
- Colons – recognition

Spelling
- Confused words – lose/loose, to/too/two, ate/eight, waste/waist
- Misspelled words

Grammar
- Conjunctions
- Present tense verbs

Vocabulary
- Compound words

Teacher Information

This health text is in the form of an explanation.

Answers

> **A** large part of our body is water**.** **I**t is needed for all the things the body has to do**.** **E**very day we *lose* a lot of water from our bodies by *sweating***,** going *to* the toilet and even when we *breathe***!** **W**e can replace this lost wate(**:**)
> - by drinking six to *eight* glasses of water each day and
> - from the foods we eat**.**
>
> **W**hen it is hot or after *exercise* we need to drink extra water**.** **W**e can live for many weeks without food, but we can only *survive* for a few days without water**.**
>
> **W**ater helps our body digest food**,** helps to control the *temperature* of the body**,** carries nutrients and *oxygen* to parts of the body**,** helps to remove *waste* and protects some parts of the body from damage**.**

1. (a) Missing punctuation and punctuation to identify is in **bold type**.
   (b) The colon is circled.
2. Spelling errors are in *italic type*.
   (a) lose, to, eight, waste
   (b) sweating, breathe, exercise, survive, temperature, oxygen
3. (a) Answers can include: when, or, and, but
   (b) Answers can include: is needed, has to do, can replace, lose, sweating, going to, breathe, is, can survive, helps digest, carries, remove, protects, eat, drinking, need to drink, can live, helps to control, helps to remove, protects
4. (a) Teacher check. Answers may include:
      anywhere, weekend, nobody, anybody, nowhere

Name _____   Date _____

Pre-Test: Addition and Subtraction
Add or subtract.

Keep your eyes open for those tricky signs!

1.
    43   63   60   55   92
    + 41   + 49   + 11   + 24   + 25

2.
    308   429   154   785   126
    + 769   + 578   + 842   + 732   + 579

3.
    1,249   9,753   36,553   99,373   511,060
    + 8,764 + 7,893 + 92,834 + 192,752 + 846,456

4.
    32   214   213   5,453   83,246
    79   566   384   1,628   76,483
    + 30   + 800   + 543   + 8,453 + 17,758

5.
    150   5,449   6,616   24,622   29,502
    130   3,908   5,431   76,556   7,574
    76   5,680   4,045   1,154   33,762
    + 97   + 5,615 5,483   9,903   93,041
                    + 2,944 + 46,147 + 23,429

6.
    24   65   53   468   578
    − 12   − 38   − 49   − 54   − 38

7.
    535   980   859   8,756   5,890
    − 526   − 578   − 589   − 4,895 − 4,895

8.
    5,890   6,789   9,835   57,897 67,893
    − 3,948 − 5,789 − 5,780 − 5,893 − 57,893

Math Connection–   © Carson-Dellosa

Water and the Body

Editing

Read the explanation.

a large part of our body is water it is needed for all the things the body has to do every day we (lose/loose) a lot of water from our bodies by swetting going (to/too/two) the toilet and even when we breeth we can replace this lost water:

- by drinking six to (ate/eight) glasses of water each day and
- from the foods we eat

when it is hot or after exerciz we need to drink extra water we can live for many weeks without food, but we can only servive for a few days without water

water helps our body digest food helps to control the temprachu of the body carries nutrients and oxyjen to parts of the body helps to remove (waste/waist) and protects some parts of the body from damage

❶ Punctuation
(a) The explanation needs 7 capital letters, 6 periods, 4 commas (used in lists) and 1 exclamation mark.

(b) Circle the colon.

❷ Spelling
(a) Circle the correct word in each bracket.

(b) 6 words are misspelled. Underline, then write the correct spelling.

_____ _____

_____ _____

_____ _____

❸ Grammar
Joining words (conjunctions) connect different ideas in a sentence or a number of short sentences into one.

(a) Write 2 conjunctions from the text.

_____ _____

Explanations are usually written in the present tense.

(b) Write 6 present tense verbs from the text.

_____ _____

_____ _____

_____ _____

❹ Vocabulary
Compound words are made by joining smaller words to make a larger word. "Without" and "everyday" (adjective) are compound words.

(a) Write 4 compound words using the words listed.

body	any	week
no	where	end

_____ _____

_____ _____

My Dance Trophy

Teacher Notes

Lesson Focus

Punctuation
- Capital letters for sentence beginnings
- Capital letters for titles
- Periods
- Grammatical commas
- Apostrophes – contractions

Spelling
- Misspelled words

Grammar
- Adjectives
- Contractions

Vocabulary
- Synonyms

Teacher Information

Descriptions describe the characteristics, components, or functions of specific living or nonliving things.

Answers

> **M**y new dance *trophy* is my most treasured *possession***.**
>
> **I** was really excited to go on stage to accept my gold *trophy***.** **I**t is bigger than any of my other *trophies* because it has a large *statue* on the top of a tap dancer wearing a black top hat**.** **T**he whole thing is about 12 *inches* tall**.** **T**he wooden base has a plaque which says "**F**irst **P**lace **U**nder-12 **Y**ears **T**ap **C**hampion."
> **I**'m going to keep it on my bedside table for a little *while* and just look at it whenever I can**.** **I** know the *statue* is really only plastic painted gold**,** but to me it**'**s the most precious thing I own!
>
> **M**om says that I can take it to school for news as long as I leave it in the room at break times**.**
>
> **M**aybe next year**,** if I practice really hard**,** there**'**ll be another one to put beside it!

1. (a) Missing punctuation is in **bold type**.
2. (a) Spelling errors are in *italic type*.
   trophy, possession, trophies, statue, inches, while
3. (a) (i) new, dance, gold (ii) black (iii) bedside
   (b) (i) I, am (ii) it, is (has) (iii) there, will (iv) are, not
   (v) you, would (had)
4. (a) Teacher check

80   Editing - Book 2   © World Teachers Press® ~ www.worldteacherspress.com

My Dance Trophy

Read the description.

my new dance trofy is my most treasured posseshon

i was really excited to go on stage to accept my gold trofy it is bigger than any of my other trofees because it has a large stachoo on the top of a tap dancer wearing a black top hat the whole thing is about 12 inches tall the wooden base has a plaque which says "first place under-12 years tap champion"
im going to keep it on my bedside table for a little wile and just look at it whenever I can i know the stachoo is really only plastic painted gold but to me its the most precious thing I own!

mom says that I can take it to school for news as long as I leave it in the room at break times

maybe next year if I practice really hard therell be another one to put beside it!

❶ Punctuation

(a) The description needs 9 capital letters for beginning sentences and 6 in a title, 7 periods, 3 commas and 3 apostrophes to show contractions.

❷ Spelling

(a) Six different words are misspelled. Write the correct spelling.

_____ _____

_____ _____

_____ _____

❸ Grammar

Descriptions include a lot of adjectives, which add meaning to nouns.

(a) Write adjectives from the text to describe these nouns:

(i) _____ trophy

(ii) _____ top hat

(iii) _____ table

Grammatical contractions are words which have been made by joining and shortening two words. An apostrophe is used in place of the missing letters.

(b) Write the words which make up these grammatical contractions.

(i) I'm _____ _____

(ii) it's _____ _____

(iii) there'll _____ _____

(iv) aren't _____ _____

(v) you'd _____ _____

❹ Vocabulary

(a) Write synonyms (words which mean the same) for these words.

(i) possession _____

(ii) base _____

(iii) precious _____

(iv) put _____

Make-a-Face Flip Book

Teacher Notes

Lesson Focus

Punctuation

- Capital letters for sentence beginnings
- Periods
- Colons – recognition

Grammar

- Verbs
- Conjunctions

Spelling

- Confused words — for/four, by/buy
- Misspelled words
- Plurals – adding "s" and "es"

Vocabulary

- Antonyms

Teacher Information

A procedure shows how something is done. Instructions are written using command verbs, usually at the beginning of sentences.

Answers

Material**s:**

- 4 sheets of *white* paper, the same size
- *colored* pencils
- stapler
- ruler
- pencil

Instruction**s:**

- **T**urn the paper lengthways, fold, then staple along the fold**.**
- **D**esign your *front* cover but *leave* the back blank**.**
- **M**easure and rule each of the six middle pages into *four* equal strips**.**
- **D**raw a *different* face on each page, keeping the features (eyes, hair, nose, etc.) on the same strip for each picture. **A**dd glasses, etc., if desired**.**
- **C**ut the six middle pages along each strip**.**
- **C**reate crazy funny faces *by* flipping *different* strips**.**

1. (a) Missing punctuation and punctuation to identify is in **bold type**.
   (b) Colons are circled.
2. (a) Spelling errors are in *italic type*.
   white, colored, front, leave, four, different, by, different
   (b) (i) staplers (ii) rulers
   (iii) brushes (iv) lunches
   (v) pencils
3. (a) Answers may include:
   Turn, staple, Design, leave, Measure, rule, Draw, keeping, Add, desired, Cut, Create, flipping
   (b) Answers can include:
   then, but, and, by
4. (a) Teacher check. Answers may include:
   (i) white   (ii) front
   (iii) crazy (iv) back
   (v) different

82   *Editing - Book 2*   © World Teachers Press® ~ www.worldteacherspress.com

Make-a-Face Flip Book

Editing

Read the procedure.

materials:
- 4 sheets of wite paper the same size
- coloured pencils
- stapler
- ruler
- pencil

instructions:
- turn the paper lengthways, fold, then staple along the fold
- design your frunt cover but leeve the back blank
- meshu and rule each of the six middle pages into for equal strips
- draw a diffrent face on each page keeping the features (eyes, hair, nose, etc.) on the same strip for each picture add glasses, etc., if desired
- cut the six middle pages along each strip
- create crazy funny faces buy flipping diffrent strips

When singular words are made plural, we can add "s" or "es"; for example, "strip**s**" and "glass**es**." We usually add "es" when we want to make the plural easier to say.

(b) Write the plural of each word.

(i) stapler _____

(ii) ruler _____

(iii) brush _____

(iv) lunch _____

(v) pencil _____

❸ *Grammar*

(a) Underline 10 verbs in the text.

(b) Write 2 different conjunctions (joining words) used in the text.

_____ _____

❹ *Vocabulary*

(a) Find opposites of these words:

(i) black _____

(ii) back _____

(iii) serious _____

(iv) front _____

(v) same _____

❶ **Punctuation**

(a) The procedure needs 9 capital letters and 7 periods.

(b) Circle the colons.

❷ **Spelling**

(a) Eight words are misspelled. Write the correct spelling.

_____ _____

_____ _____

_____ _____

_____ _____

Too Many Dogs

Teacher Notes

Lesson Focus

Punctuation

- Capital letters for sentence beginnings
- Capital letters for proper nouns
- Capital letters for the pronoun "I"
- Periods
- Grammatical commas

Spelling

- Confused words: writing/righting, two/to, poor/pore, sum/some
- Misspelled words

Grammar

- Apostrophes for possession

Vocabulary

- Synonyms

Teacher Information

Expositions are written or spoken to persuade others to think or do something. Expositions use persuasive language.

Answers

> **D**ear **M**r. **J**ames:
>
> **I** am *writing* to request that the city takes *some* action about my neighbor's dogs**.**
>
> **C**ity regulations permit only *two* dogs**,** but my neighbor at 7 **H**ill **S**treet has at *least* six**.**
>
> **T**he dogs are neglected**. T**hey are enclosed in a small area and never taken for walks**. I** suspect that they are not *fed* regularly**,** *because* they look very thin**. A**nother problem is the *noise* they make**. S**ometimes they bark all day and they *often* cry at *night***.**
>
> **A**part from the noise**,** which keeps us awake**, I** am concerned for the welfare of these *poor* animals**. I**mmediate action is required**.**
>
> **Y**ours *sincerely,*
>
> **M**ary **B**lack

1. (a) Missing punctuation is **bold type**.
2. (a) Spelling errors are in *italic type*.
   writing, some, two, least, fed, because, noise, often, night, poor, sincerely
3. (a) Teacher check
   (b) It is needed for the possessive. The dogs belong to the neighbor.
   (c) One neighbor
4. (a) Teacher check

Too Many Dogs

Editing

Read the exposition which is in the form of a letter.

dear mr. james:

i am (writing/righting) to request that the city takes (sum/some) action about my neighbor's dogs

city regulations permit only (to/two) dogs but my neighbor at 7 hill street has at (least/leest) six

the dogs are neglected they are enclosed in a small area and never taken for walks i suspect that they are not (feed/fed) regularly (because/becos) they look very thin another problem is the (niose/noise) they make sometimes they bark all day and they (ofen/often) cry at (nite/night)

apart from the noise which keeps us awake i am concerned for the welfare of these (poor/pore) animals immediate action is required

yours (sincerly/sincerely),

mary black

❶ Punctuation

(a) The exposition needs 6 capital letters for proper nouns, 3 for the word "I," 9 for sentence beginnings, 9 periods and 4 commas.

❷ Spelling

(a) Circle the correct word in each bracket.

❸ Grammar

(a) Find an owner or owners for these things. The apostrophe is written directly after the owner or owners. One has been done.

(i) books *The school's books*

(ii) shoes _____

(iii) pets _____

(iv) wheels _____

(b) Why is there an apostrophe in "neighbor's"?

_____

(c) Is Mary Black writing to complain about one or more than one neighbor? (Look at the apostrophe.)

_____

❹ Vocabulary

(a) Find synonyms for these words.

(i) request _____

(ii) thin _____

(iii) enclosed _____

(iv) suspect _____

(v) required _____

Sabre-Toothed Cat

Teacher Notes

Lesson Focus

Punctuation
- Capital letters for sentence beginnings
- Periods
- Exclamation marks
- Grammatical commas

Grammar
- Adjectives
- Verb tenses – past tense

Spelling
- Misspelled words
- Suffixes – doubling consonants

Vocabulary
- Similes

Teacher Information

This descriptive report presents clear facts about the sabre-toothed cat.

Answers

> **T**he sabre-toothed cat became extinct about 10,000 years ago**.** **M**any *different* species existed but all had one thing in *common*; each had two long, pointed upper teeth shaped like a sabre (curved sword)**.**
>
> **F**ossil remains suggest that the sabre-toothed cat was not built for speed**.** **I**t was powerful and heavy with relatively short limbs**.** **T**o capture its prey, the sabre-toothed cat would have either stalked or attacked large animals from a *hiding* place rather than chasing them**.** **W**hen it caught an animal**,** its enormous teeth would tear a ripping wound into the throat or *belly***.** **I**t would then let go of the animal and let it bleed to death**.** **I**f it kept *biting* its prey**,** its teeth could break, as they were fairly fragile**.** **N**umerous *fossil* fragments of broken teeth have been found**.**
>
> **W**hat a nightmare for a dentist**!**

1. (a) Missing punctuation is in **bold type**.
2. (a) Spelling errors are in *italic type*.
    different, common, hiding, belly, biting, fossil
   (b) (i) chasing (ii) ripping (iii) running (iv) smiling
3. (a) long, pointed, upper, enormous, fragile, broken
   (b) stalked, attacked
4. (a) Teacher check

Sabre-Toothed Cat

Editing

Read the report.

the sabre-toothed cat became extinct about 10,000 years ago many diferent species existed but all had one thing in comon; each had two long, pointed upper teeth shaped like a sabre (curved sword)

fossil remains suggest that the sabre-toothed cat was not built for speed it was powerful and heavy with relatively short limbs to capture its prey, the sabre-toothed cat would have either stalked or attacked large animals from a hidding place rather than chasing them when it caught an animal its enormous teeth would tear a ripping wound into the throat or bely it would then let go of the animal and let it bleed to death if it kept bitting its prey its teeth could break, as they were fairly fragile numerous fosil fragments of broken teeth have been found

what a nightmare for a dentist

❶ Punctuation

(a) The report needs 10 capital letters, 9 periods, 1 exclamation mark and 2 commas in paragraph 2.

❷ Spelling

(a) Six words have been misspelled. Write the correct spelling.

_____   _____

_____   _____

_____   _____

*When adding a suffix such as "ing" to a word, the final consonant is doubled only if you want to keep the vowel short; for example, "hop – ho**pp**ing," "hope – hoping."*

(b) Add "ing" to these words.

(i) chase _____

(ii) rip _____

(iii) run _____

(iv) smile _____

❸ Grammar

Adjectives describe nouns.

(a) Write 5 adjectives that describe the sabre-toothed cat's teeth.

_____

_____

_____

(b) Write two words in the past tense in the report that end in "ed."

_____

❹ Vocabulary

The sabre-toothed cat gets it name because its teeth are shaped "like a sabre." This is a simile. Similes compare one thing to another.

(a) Complete each of these similies.

(i) The cat's fur is as

_____

(ii) To prowl like a

_____

Lifecycle of a Butterfly

Teacher Notes

Lesson Focus

Punctuation
- Capital letters for sentence beginnings
- Periods
- Grammatical commas

Spelling
- Confused words – witch/which, for/four, its/it's
- Misspelled words
- Plurals: change from "y" to "i" and add "es"

Grammar
- Nouns
- Adjectives

Vocabulary
- Synonyms

Teacher Information

Explanations analyze how things work, or how or why things happen.

Answers

The lifecycle of a butterfly is an example of metamorphosis, *which* means "complete change." **T**he metamorphosis of a butterfly happens in four stages**.**

Butterfly eggs are laid on the leaves of plants. **T**hese leaves provide food for the second stage of development**.**

The caterpillar emerges from the egg and begins to devour the plant. **I**t grows rapidly and sheds its outer skin as many as *four* times before it is ready for the chrysalis stage**.**

After about four weeks**,** the caterpillar molts one more time before *attaching* itself to a branch for support. **I**t weaves a silken cocoon for protection and remains dormant until it is ready for the final change**.**

At last**,** the butterfly is ready to emerge. **I**t forces itself out of *its* silken cocoon**,** flaps its wings and takes to the air**.**

1. (a) Missing punctuation is in **bold type**.
2. (a) Spelling errors are in *italic type*. which, four, attaching, its
   (b) (i) babies (ii) parties (iii) stories
3. (a) (i) cocoon (ii) stage (iii) skin (iv) change
4. (a) (i) inactive – dormant
   (ii) appears – emerges
   (iii) eat hungrily – devour
   (iv) swiftly – rapidly
   (v) phase – stage

Lifecycle of a Butterfly

Read the explanation.

the lifecycle of a butterfly is an example of metamorphosis (which/witch) means "complete change" the metamorphosis of a butterfly happens in four stages

butterfly eggs are laid on the leaves of plants these leaves provide food for the second **stage** of development

the caterpillar **emerges** from the egg and begins to **devour** the plant it grows **rapidly** and sheds its outer skin as many as (for/four) times before it is ready for the chrysalis stage

after about four weeks the caterpillar molts one more time before (attatching/attaching) itself to a branch for support it weaves a silken cocoon for protection and remains **dormant** until it is ready for the final change

at last the butterfly is ready to emerge it forces itself out of (its/it's) silken cocoon flaps its wings and takes to the air

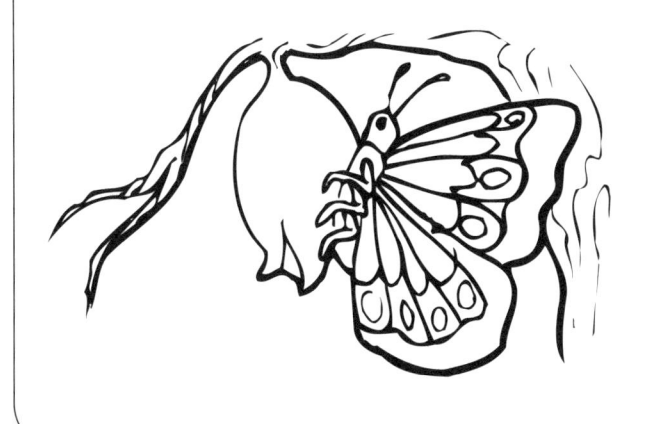

❶ Punctuation
(a) The explanation needs 10 capital letters, 10 periods and 4 commas.

❷ Spelling
(a) Circle the correct word in each bracket.

The plural of many words is made simply by adding the letter "s," but others have different rules; for example, "one butterfly, two butterflies." The rule is change the "y" to "i" and add "es."

(b) Write the plural of these words:

   (i) baby _____

   (ii) party _____

   (iii) story _____

❸ Grammar
(a) Write the nouns these adjectives describe.

   (i) silken _____

   (ii) second _____

   (iii) outer _____

   (iv) final _____

❹ Vocabulary
Synonyms are words that have the same or similar meanings.

(a) Match these words with their synonyms, highlighted in the text.

   (i) inactive _____

   (ii) appears _____

   (iii) eat hungrily _____

   (iv) swiftly _____

   (v) phase _____

Save Our Water

Teacher Notes

Lesson Focus

Punctuation

- Capital letters for sentence beginnings
- Capital letters for proper nouns
- Periods
- Exclamation marks

Spelling

- Confused words – be/bee, for/fore, shore/sure
- Misspelled words
- Doubling consonants to keep vowels short

Grammar

- Verb tense

Vocabulary

- Synonyms

Teacher Information

An exposition is written or spoken to persuade people to think or do something.

Answers

Water is our most precious resource and it must *be* preserved**.**

Worldwide shortages will be a serious problem in the future unless we do something to reduce the amount of water we use now**. T**his is not something *for* future generations to worry about, it is our problem and we need to take immediate action**.**

Water is essential for life**. W**e need water for *drinking*, *washing* and producing food**. W**e simply cannot do without it**.**

Only a small amount of all the water on the **E**arth is usable fresh water**. W**e need to make *sure* that the quality of our water is protected**. P**ollution must be *stopped*.

In our homes and gardens, we can all help to preserve water by *cutting* down on the amount we use every day**. W**e can use less garden fertilizer and detergent**.**

Water conservation is our problem and we must deal with it NOW**!**

1. (a) Missing punctuation is in **bold type**.
   (b) Teacher check; to add emphasis
2. (a) Spelling errors are in *italic type*.
       be, for, drinking, washing, sure, stopped, cutting
   (b) (i) swimming (ii) shopping
       (iii) shutting (iv) slamming
3. (a) (i) slipped (ii) slapped
       (iii) stopped
4. (a) (i) precious – valuable
       (ii) reduce – lower
       (iii) essential – necessary
       (iv) produce – make
       (v) preserve – save

Save Our Water

Read the exposition.

water is our most precious resource and it must (be/bee) preserved

worldwide shortages will be a serious problem in the future unless we do something to reduce the amount of water we use now this is not something (fore/for) future generations to worry about, it is our problem and we need to take immediate action

water is essential for life we need water for (drincking/drinking), (washing/woshing) and producing food we simply cannot do without it

only a small amount of all the water on the earth is usable fresh water we need to make (sure/shore) that the quality of our water is protected pollution must be (stopped/stoped)

in our homes and gardens, we can all help to preserve water by (cuting/cutting) down on the amount we use every day we can use less garden fertilizer and detergent

water conservation is our problem and we must deal with it NOW!

Editing

❶ Punctuation

(a) The exposition needs 13 capital letters and 11 periods.

(b) Why is there an exclamation mark after "NOW"?

_____

❷ Spelling

(a) Circle the correct word in each bracket.

When adding a suffix, double the final consonant to keep the vowel short; for example, "stopping."

(b) Add "ing" to these words

(i) swim _____

(ii) shop _____

(iii) shut _____

(iv) slam _____

❸ Grammar

(a) Add "ed" to these words to change them from present to past tense.

(i) slip _____

(ii) slap _____

(iii) stop _____

❹ Vocabulary

(a) Match these synonyms.

(i) precious • • save

(ii) reduce • • lower

(iii) essential • • valuable

(iv) produce • • make

(v) preserve • • necessary

Black Mamba

Teacher Notes

Lesson Focus

Punctuation

- Capital letters for sentence beginnings
- Capital letters used for proper nouns
- Periods
- Apostrophes for possession

Spelling

- Confused words – to/two/too, wholes/holes, pray/prey, pears/pairs
- Misspelled words

Grammar

- Adjectives
- Apostrophes for possession
- Contractions

Vocabulary

- Shortened word forms

Teacher Information

Reports give facts clearly without unneccessary information or opinions.

Answers

> **T**he black mamba is the deadliest snake in the world**.** It's **S**outh **A**frica**'**s most *poisonous* snake**.** **I**t can grow up to lengths of 13 feet and can travel at *speeds* of up *to* 12 miles per hour**.** **T**he black mamba gets its name from the inside lining of its mouth, which is purple-black**.** **I**t shows its mouth when it feels threatened**.** **I**t feeds on small *mammals* and birds and is able to eat its *prey* whole**.**
>
> **I**t likes to sleep in hollow trees or *holes* in the ground**.** **F**emale mambas can lay from six to seventeen eggs, which hatch three months later**.** **B**lack mambas are found in *pairs* or small groups**.** **T**he *venom* of the mamba can kill almost anything**.**

1. (a) Missing punctuation is in **bold type**.
2. Spelling errors are in *italic type*.
   - (a) to, prey, holes, pairs
   - (b) poisonous, speeds, mammals, venom
3. (a) (i) That snake's eggs hatched. (ii) Its mouth's lining is purple-black.
   (iii) The black mamba's venom can kill. (iv) Black mambas' nests can be in tree hollows.
   (b) Answers will include: black, deadliest, poisonous
   (c) The sentence is underlined.
   It's South Africa's most poisonous snake.
   (d) (i) It's (ii) Its (iii) its
4. (a) (i) 13 ft. (ii) 12 mph (iii) S.A. (iv) Aust.

Black Mamba

Editing

Read the report.

the black mamba is the deadliest snake in the world it's south africas most poisonus snake it can grow up to lengths of 13 feet and can travel at speads of up (to/too/two) 12 miles per hour the black mamba gets its name from the inside lining of its mouth, which is purple-black it shows its mouth when it feels threatened it feeds on small mammels and birds and is able to eat its (pray/prey) whole

it likes to sleep in hollow trees or (wholes/holes) in the ground female mambas can lay from six to seventeen eggs, which hatch three months later black mambas are found in (pairs/pears) or small groups the venim of the mamba can kill almost anything

❶ Punctuation

(a) The report needs 10 capital letters for sentence beginnings, 2 for proper nouns, 10 periods and 1 apostrophe.

❷ Spelling

(a) Circle the correct word in each bracket.

(b) Four words have been misspelled. Write the correct spelling.

_____   _____

_____   _____

❸ Grammar

An apostrophe is written after the owner or owners to show possession.

(a) Add the apostrophes.

(i) That snakes eggs hatched.

(ii) Its mouths lining is purple-black.

(iii) The black mambas venom can kill.

(iv) Black mambas nests can be in tree hollows.

(b) Write two adjectives from the text describing black mambas.

_____   _____

"It's" is a contraction and can only be used in place of the words "it is" and "it has."

(c) Underline the sentence with this contraction.

(d) Circle the correct spelling.

(i) (Its/It's) poisonous.

(ii) (It's/Its) venom is deadly.

(iii) It eats (it's/its) prey.

❹ Vocabulary

(a) Write shortened forms for:

(i) 13 feet   _____

(ii) 12 miles per hour _____

(iii) South Africa   _____

(iv) Australia   _____

A Warrior Queen's Dilemma

Teacher Notes

Lesson Focus

Punctuation

- Capital letters for sentence beginnings
- Periods
- Apostrophes for contractions
- Grammatical commas
- Direct speech
- Exclamation marks

Spelling

- Misspelled words

Grammar

- Collective nouns
- Verbs
- Adverbs

Teacher Information

A narrative tells a story in a sequence of events often involving fictitious characters.

Answers

Callista**,** warrior queen**,** looked anxious as she quietly surveyed her kingdom in ancient Britain.

"<u>I have to think of a plan**,**</u>**"** she said to Teldak, her trusted *adviser*. **"**<u>The harvest was poor because we**'**ve had no rain and the gangs of bandits are attacking the outer villages. Our people need our help</u>**!"**

The following day, Callista called together the village leaders to present ideas and discuss solutions to their problems. Finally, it was decided to use the farm *laborers* to construct a protective barrier on the outskirts of the kingdom to deter the bandits until peaceful *negotiations* could be arranged. As well**,** irrigation channels were to be dug to the river to divert water for crops**.** **T**rade contacts were also to be *established* with the Shedrons, who lived on the other side of the mountain.

"<u>At last**,** I feel like we**'**re doing something positive. I see a bright future for our people</u>**!"** she announced.

1. (a) Missing punctuation is in **bold type**.
   (b) Direct speech is <u>underlined</u>.
2. (a) Spelling errors are in *italic type*.
       adviser, laborers, negotiations, established
3. (a) gangs
   (b) Teacher check; answers may include:
       (i) troop, army, platoon
       (ii) herd, mob
       (iii) flock
       (iv) group, crowd
   (c) (verb) looked; surveyed, (adverb) quietly
   (d) Teacher check

A Warrior Queen's Dilemma

Read the narrative.

Callista warrior queen looked anxious as she quietly surveyed her kingdom in ancient Britain.

I have to think of a plan, she said to Teldak, her trusted advisir. The harvest was poor because weve had no rain and the gangs of bandits are attacking the outer villages. Our people need our help

The following day, Callista called together the village leaders to present ideas and discuss solutions to their problems. Finally, it was decided to use the farm labourers to construct a protective barrier on the outskirts of the kingdom to deter the bandits until peaceful negociations could be arranged. As well irrigation channels were to be dug to the river to divert water for crops trade contacts were also to be estableshed with the Shedrons, who lived on the other side of the mountain.

At last I feel like were doing something positive. I see a bright future for our people she announced.

Editing

1 Punctuation
(a) The narrative needs 1 period and 1 capital letter, 2 exclamation marks, 2 apostrophes for contractions and 3 grammatical commas.

(b) Underline the direct speech and write the 3 missing sets of quotation marks.

2 Spelling
(a) Write the correct spelling of 4 misspelled words.

_____   _____

_____   _____

3 Grammar
(a) Write 1 collective noun from the second paragraph.

_____

(b) Write collective nouns for these groups.

   (i)   a _____ of soldiers

   (ii) a _____ of cattle

   (iii) a _____ of birds

   (iv) a _____ of people

(c) Write 1 verb and 1 adverb from the first paragraph.

   (verb)   _____

   (adverb) _____

(d) Think of an appropriate adverb for each verb.

   (i)   attacked   _____

   (ii) discuss   _____

   (iii) construct _____

Pennies and Pencils

Teacher Notes

Lesson Focus

Punctuation
- Capital letters for sentence beginnings
- Capital letters used for proper nouns
- Periods
- Grammatical commas
- Apostrophes to show possession

Spelling
- Misspelled words
- Plurals – change "y" to "i"

Grammar
- Adjectives
- Adverbs

Writing
- Paragraphs

Teacher Information

A book review is a type of report.

Answers

Pennies and Pencils, written by **E**leanor **B**aker, is a story of a ten-year-old girl called **C**hristine who must deal with the fact that her grandmother, **J**udith, is dying of cancer**. S**he is very upset but *decides* that she can remember her grandmother forever by writing down her grandmother**'**s *memories* in a book, which she has called *Pennies and Pencils***. B**y talking to her grandmother and recording her life *experiences*, she learns a lot about her grandmother**'**s life as a girl and becomes even closer to her at the end of her life**.**

This book, although dealing with a difficult subject, includes some amusing incidents of **J**udith**'**s life in the 1950s**. I**t shows her *mischievous* days as a young girl and gives an insight into life at the time**.**

The illustrations**,** by **C**hris **J**ohns**,** are very detailed, colorful and enlightening**. T**hey contribute significantly to this lovely story which celebrates life**.**

1. Missing punctuation is in **bold type**.
2. (a) (i) cherries (ii) bunnies (iii) stories (iv) families
   (b) Spelling errors are in *italic type*.
       decides, memories, experiences, mischievous
3. (a) (i) lovely (ii) significantly
4. (a) Paragraph 3 provides information about the illustrations.

Pennies and Pencils

Editing

Read this report in the form of a book review.

Pennies and Pencils, written by eleanor baker, *is a story of a ten-year-old girl called* christine *who must deal with the fact that her grandmother, judith, is dying of cancer she is very upset but desides that she can remember her grandmother forever by writing down her grandmothers memries in a book, which she has called* Pennies and Pencils *by talking to her grandmother and recording her life expereinces, she learns a lot about her grandmothers life as a girl and becomes even closer to her at the end of her life*

this book, although dealing with a difficult subject, includes some amusing incidents of judiths life in the 1950s it shows her mischeivous days as a young girl and gives an insight into life at the time

the illustrations by chris johns are very detailed, colorful and enlightening they contribute significantly to this lovely story which celebrates life

❶ Punctuation

(a) The report needs 13 capital letters (7 for proper nouns), 7 periods and 2 commas in the last paragraph.

(b) Put in 3 apostrophes needed to show possession.

❷ Spelling

When we change singular nouns, such as "memory," to plural, we change the "y" to "i" and add "es"; for example, "memory – memories."

(a) Change these singular nouns to plural using the spelling rule.

   (i) cherry _____

   (ii) bunny _____

   (iii) story _____

   (iv) family _____

(b) Four words are misspelled. Write the correct spelling.

_____   _____

_____   _____

❸ Grammar

Adjectives describe nouns. Adverbs add meaning to verbs and often end in "ly."

(a) Underline the 2 "ly" words in the text. Which one is:

   (i) an adjective? _____

   (ii) an adverb? _____

❹ Writing

Paragraphs introduce a new idea.

(a) What information is given in paragraph 3?

_____

The Curse of the Mummy

Teacher Notes

Lesson Focus

Punctuation

- Capital letters for sentence beginnings
- Capital letters for proper nouns
- Periods
- Grammatical commas
- Direct speech
- Apostrophes for contractions
- Apostrophes for possession

Spelling

- Misspelled words

Grammar

- Adjectives
- Indefinite article "a" or "an"

Teacher Information

This newspaper report is a recount which includes the following characteristics:

- a headline (to capture attention, short),
- a lead sentence (similar to a headline only more detailed to entice the reader to continue),
- details (who, what, where, when, why—it may also include eyewitnesses),
- a conclusion.

Answers

A theatrical stunt at the **S**tate **M**useum yesterday went horribly wrong when a group of schoolchildren *thought* they were being attacked by a 4,000-year-old mummy**.**

The management had decided to use an actor to come *out* of a fake sarcophagus in the middle of their **E**gyptian exhibition**.**

The guide on (yesterday's) *tour* said that he simply forgot to tell the children what was happening.

"**I**t was a difficult *group*₍,₎" he said**.** "**T**hey were a *noisy* bunch of **G**rade 5 children₍,₎ and they distracted me**."**

As the children entered the room₍,₎ the actor₍,₎ dressed as a mummy₍,₎ emerged from the sarcophagus₍,₎ amid screams of terror from the students**. O**ne child fainted**. T**he actor was injured when he tripped over trying to unravel some of his bandages to let the children know he was an actor**.**

"**I**t was so *scary*₍,₎" one child reported**.** "**I**t was worse when he started undoing his bandages₍,₎ *because* I (didn't) know *what* would be underneath**."**

The museum curator commented that this was the first time *something* like this had happened during the four weeks the stunt had been used**. A**ngry parents₍,₎ however₍,₎ are threatening to sue.

1. (a) Missing punctuation and punctuation to identify is in **bold type**.
   (b) The 10 commas are circled.
   (c) The two words with apostrophes are circled.
       yesterday's – possession
       didn't – contraction
   (d) Direct speech is underlined. Speech marks are in **bold type**.
2. (a) Spelling errors are in *italic type*.
       thought, out, tour, group, noisy, because, what, something
3. (a) (i) theatrical
       (ii) Egyptian
       (iii) noisy
       (iv) angry
   (b) (i) an actor
       (ii) an injury
       (iii) a room

The Curse of the Mummy

Editing

Read the newspaper report.

a theatrical stunt at the state museum yesterday went horribly wrong when a group of schoolchildren thort they were being attacked by a 4000-year-old mummy

the management had decided to use an actor to come owt of a fake sarcophagus in the middle of their egyptian exhibition

the guide on yesterdays tor said that he simply forgot to tell the children what was happening

it was a difficult groop, he said they were a noise bunch of grade 5 children, and they distracted me

as the children entered the room, the actor, dressed as a mummy, emerged from the sarcophagus, amid screams of terror from the students one child fainted the actor was injured when he tripped over trying to unravel some of his bandages to let the children know he was an actor

it was so scary, one child reported it was worse when he started undoing his bandages,
becors I didnt know whot would be underneath

the museum curator commented that this was the first time somethink like this had happened during the four weeks the stunt had been used angry parents, however, are threatening to sue

❶ Punctuation
(a) The report needs 4 capital letters used for proper nouns, 12 at the beginning of sentences and 12 periods.

(b) Circle 10 commas.

(c) Find and circle 2 apostrophes—one used to show possession and one for a contraction.

(d) Underline the direct speech and put in the missing speech marks.

❷ Spelling
(a) Highlight the 8 misspelled words and write them correctly.

_____ _____

_____ _____

_____ _____

_____ _____

❸ Grammar
(a) Write the adjectives used in the text to describe these nouns.

(i) _____ stunt

(ii) _____ exhibition

(iii) _____ bunch

(iv) _____ parents

Nouns starting with a vowel sound need "an" instead of "a."

(b) Complete these.

(i) _____ actor

(ii) _____ injury

(iii) _____ room

The Storm

Teacher Notes

Lesson Focus

Punctuation

- Capital letters for proper nouns
- Apostrophes for possession
- Grammatical commas
- Direct speech

Grammar

- Adjectives

Spelling

- Confused words – sea/see, reigns/rains/reins, pale/pail, their/there/they're
- Misspelled words

Vocabulary

- Shortened forms

Teacher Information

A narrative tells a story in a sequence of events often invoving fictitious characters.

Answers

> A sleek white sailboat bounces on a stormy sea. The black sky is home to sharp *lightning* bolts and rumbling thunder.
>
> The captain ties up any equipment which is rolling about and prepares to ride out the storm. Dr. **S**awbones and an old priest**,** Fr. **C**elestial**,** huddle fearfully in their life jackets below decks. The pounding of the boat**'**s bow against the *monstrous* waves is weakening the boat and may lead the captain to send out an SOS.
>
> After endless hours of rocking and swaying, the movement of the boat eases and silence reigns. The thankful *passengers* venture to the deck to greet a pale blue skyline and a restful sea.
>
> **"**I am always amazed how powerful nature is!**"** sighs the relieved captain.

1. (a) Missing punctuation is in **bold type**.
   (b) (i) The captain's ship.
       (ii) Some passengers' luggage.
2. (a) Spelling errors are in *italic type*.
   lightning, monstrous, passengers
   (b) (i) see   (ii) rains, reins   (iii) pail   (iv) there/they're
3. (a) Teacher check; answers may include: sleek, white, stormy, black, sharp, rumbling, life, monstrous, endless, thankful, pale (blue), restful, relieved
4. (a) (i) Doctor   (ii) Father   (iii) Save Our Souls

The Storm

Editing

Read the narrative.

A sleek white sailboat bounces on a stormy sea. The black sky is home to sharp lightening bolts and rumbling thunder.

The captain ties up any equipment which is rolling about and prepares to ride out the storm. Dr. sawbones and an old priest Fr. celestial huddle fearfully in their life jackets below decks. The pounding of the boats bow against the monstrus waves is weakening the boat and may lead the captain to send out an SOS.

After endless hours of rocking and swaying, the movement of the boat eases and silence reigns. The thankful passingers venture to the deck to greet a pale blue skyline and a restful sea.

I am always amazed how powerful nature is! sighs the relieved captain.

❶ Punctuation

(a) The narrative needs 2 capital letters for proper nouns, 1 apostrophe for possession, 2 grammatical commas and 1 set of quotation (speech) marks.

Apostrophes for possession are written after the owners.

(b) Add apostrophes.

(i) The captains ship.

(ii) Some passengers luggage.

❷ Spelling

(a) Write the correct spelling of 3 misspelled words.

_____

_____

(b) Write words which sound the same but are spelled differently.

(i) sea _____

(ii) reigns _____

(iii) pale _____

(iv) their _____

❸ Grammar

(a) Circle any 8 adjectives in the text.

❹ Vocabulary

(a) Underline 3 shortened forms and write the complete words for each.

_____

_____

_____

Drink Water!

Teacher Notes

Lesson Focus

Punctuation
- Capital letters for sentence beginnings
- Periods
- Exclamation marks
- Apostrophes for possession
- Grammatical commas

Grammar
- Pronouns

Spelling
- Misspelled words
- Plurals – change "y" to "i" before adding "es"

Vocabulary
- Enrichment – word definitions

Teacher Information

This exposition has been written to persuade the reader that drinking water is essential for a healthy body.

Answers

We need to drink water**.**

In an emergency, we could survive for a few days without food, but without water, our bodies would be unable to function**. K**eep a glass by the tap to remind you to "take a drink**.**"

We need to drink *enough* water**. I**t is recommended that we drink one litre of water each day**. T**his amount should be drunk throughout the day, rather than all at once**.**

It is *important* that we drink water before we feel thirsty**. T**hirst is the body**'**s way of telling us that the process of dehydration has already started**. C**arry a bottle of water with you at all times and remember, "take a drink."

We need to drink water before, during and after exercise, to *replace* the fluid lost through sweating**.**

We need to drink water in *addition* to other drinks because they may contain substances which increase thirst**.**

For a healthy body, drink water**!**

1. (a) Missing punctuation is in **bold type**.
   (b) The 8 commas are circled.
2. (a) Spelling errors are in *italic type*.
   enough, important, replace, addition
   (b) (i) curries   (ii) babies
   (iii) berries   (iv) trophies
3. (a) our, it, you, they
4. (a) (i) function – work
   (ii) recommended – suggested as being good
   (iii) substances – anything of which a thing is made (analogy: ingredients in a cake mixture)
   (iv) dehydration – losing water

Drink Water!

Read this exposition.

we need to drink water

in an emergency, we could survive for a few days without food, but without water, our bodies would be unable to **function** keep a glass by the tap to remind you to "take a drink"

we need to drink enuf water it is **recommended** that we drink one litre of water each day this amount should be drunk throughout the day, rather than all at once

it is inportant that we drink water before we feel thirsty thirst is the bodys way of telling us that the process of **dehydration** has already started carry a bottle of water with you at all times and remember, "take a drink"

we need to drink water before, during and after exercise, to replace the fluid lost through sweating

we need to drink water in addishun to other drinks because they may contain **substances** which increase thirst

for a healthy body, drink water

Editing

❶ Punctuation

(a) The exposition needs 12 capital letters, 11 periods, 1 exclamation mark and 1 apostrophe for possession.

(b) Circle the commas. How many are there? _____

❷ Spelling

(a) 4 words are misspelled. Write the correct spelling.

_____   _____

_____   _____

When we change singular nouns such as "body" to plural, we change the "y" to "i" before adding "es." For example, body – bodies.

(b) Change these nouns to plurals.

(i) curry _____

(ii) baby _____

(iii) berry _____

(iv) trophy _____

❸ Grammar

(a) Write 3 pronouns used in the text.

_____

❹ Vocabulary

(a) Find the meaning of the words in bold print.

(i) _____

(ii) _____

(iii) _____

(iv) _____